Thomas Heinis

Workflow-based Services

Thomas Heinis

Workflow-based Services
Infrastructure for Scientific Applications

Südwestdeutscher Verlag für Hochschulschriften

Impressum / Imprint
Bibliografische Information der Deutschen Nationalbibliothek: Die Deutsche Nationalbibliothek verzeichnet diese Publikation in der Deutschen Nationalbibliografie; detaillierte bibliografische Daten sind im Internet über http://dnb.d-nb.de abrufbar.
Alle in diesem Buch genannten Marken und Produktnamen unterliegen warenzeichen-, marken- oder patentrechtlichem Schutz bzw. sind Warenzeichen oder eingetragene Warenzeichen der jeweiligen Inhaber. Die Wiedergabe von Marken, Produktnamen, Gebrauchsnamen, Handelsnamen, Warenbezeichnungen u.s.w. in diesem Werk berechtigt auch ohne besondere Kennzeichnung nicht zu der Annahme, dass solche Namen im Sinne der Warenzeichen- und Markenschutzgesetzgebung als frei zu betrachten wären und daher von jedermann benutzt werden dürften.

Bibliographic information published by the Deutsche Nationalbibliothek: The Deutsche Nationalbibliothek lists this publication in the Deutsche Nationalbibliografie; detailed bibliographic data are available in the Internet at http://dnb.d-nb.de.
Any brand names and product names mentioned in this book are subject to trademark, brand or patent protection and are trademarks or registered trademarks of their respective holders. The use of brand names, product names, common names, trade names, product descriptions etc. even without a particular marking in this work is in no way to be construed to mean that such names may be regarded as unrestricted in respect of trademark and brand protection legislation and could thus be used by anyone.

Verlag / Publisher:
Südwestdeutscher Verlag für Hochschulschriften
ist ein Imprint der / is a trademark of
OmniScriptum GmbH & Co. KG
Heinrich-Böcking-Str. 6-8, 66121 Saarbrücken, Deutschland / Germany
Email: info@svh-verlag.de

Herstellung: siehe letzte Seite /
Printed at: see last page
ISBN: 978-3-8381-1608-2

Zugl. / Approved by: Zürich, ETH, Diss., 2009

Copyright © 2010 OmniScriptum GmbH & Co. KG
Alle Rechte vorbehalten. / All rights reserved. Saarbrücken 2010

Contents

1. **Introduction**   1

I. Workflow As A Service   4

2. **Introduction**   5
   - 2.1. Introduction 5
   - 2.2. Related Work 7
3. **An Interface for Stateful Computations**   8
   - 3.1. Workflow Model 8
   - 3.2. Mapping Workflows to WS-Resources 9
   - 3.3. Applications 12
4. **Design**   15
   - 4.1. JOpera Workflow Execution Engine 15
   - 4.2. Mirrored Architecture 16
   - 4.3. Embedded Architecture 23
   - 4.4. Comparison 25
5. **Conclusions**   29

II. Autonomic Workflow Execution   30

6. **Introduction**   31
   - 6.1. Motivation 31
   - 6.2. Related Work 32
7. **Background**   35
   - 7.1. Workflow Execution Engine Architecture 35
   - 7.2. Performance Evaluation 38
8. **Autonomic Controller**   43
   - 8.1. Autonomic Capabilities 43
   - 8.2. Autonomic Workflow Execution 48
   - 8.3. Conclusions 53

9. Basic Policies — 55
- 9.1. Threshold-Based Policies 55
- 9.2. Evaluation 57
- 9.3. Conclusions 64

10. Zero Configuration Policies — 65
- 10.1. PID Controller Policy 65
- 10.2. Balancing (Zero-Configuration) Policy 67
- 10.3. Evaluation 69
- 10.4. Conclusions 76

11. Conclusions — 77

III. Data Lineage Tracking — 79

12. Data Lineage Tracking — 80
- 12.1. Introduction 80
- 12.2. Related Work 82

13. Efficient Lineage Storage — 83
- 13.1. Workflow Based Data Lineage 83
- 13.2. Encoding DAGs With Intervals 86
- 13.3. Transformation Algorithm 89
- 13.4. Evaluation 97

14. Sisyphus Use Case — 104
- 14.1. Project Background 104
- 14.2. Lineage in the TPP 107
- 14.3. Encoding Approaches 111
- 14.4. Encoding Evaluation 117
- 14.5. Sisyphus 125

15. Conclusions — 126

16. Conclusions — 128

Bibliography — 131

1. Introduction

The process of scientific discovery has changed significantly in recent years. With the use of computational means, the face of experiments in many scientific disciplines like biology, physics, astronomy etc. has changed. Experiments are no longer only executed by retrieving data from instruments and analyzing it on paper or in simplistic tools. Instead, in case of many experiments, obtaining the raw experiment data from instruments is only the first step. What follows the data acquisition phase is data processing with computationally intense and long running processing pipelines.

The trend to support traditional science with computational tools has simplified as well as sped up many experiments and has made others possible. Analyzing protein interaction networks for instance has been sped up substantially. The results produced in the context of a Ph.D analyzing protein interaction in the 1990s can now be obtained in a few days. High throughput proteomics on the other hand has only been enabled recently by the use of mass spectrometry and computational processing pipelines.

With this trend, the traditional research cycle which used to be "hypothesis → experiment → analysis → publication" has evolved into "hypothesis → experiment → data organization → data processing → analysis → publication", where the steps of data organization, data processing and analysis often need to be repeated.

The traditional research cycle did only require the scientist to have domain specific knowledge. With the two new phases of data organization and data processing scientists also require knowledge, even if only limited, on how to organize data, build processing tools and visualize results. Building infrastructure and tools to support scientists is very challenging and entails interesting computer science research problems.

The work presented in this book attempts to address some of the challenges arising from supporting scientists in building processing pipelines to process their raw data from instruments. With this it tries to provide them with tools that will help speeding up and enabling the process of scientific discovery while relieving the scientist from computer science concerns, letting him focus on his science.

There is a consensus in the community that such processing pipelines can and should be implemented as workflows. Doing so helps to develop, maintain and reuse these data processing pipelines. Using workflow tools, scientists can easily and often visually develop the processing pipeline for their needs by orchestrating existing tools - a stark contrast to having to glue virtually incompatible interfaces together with shell scripts.

Using workflows for scientific computations however also introduces new research challenges. This book is based on the published results of our work in the area of scientific workflows. It addresses three problems in the area of scientific workflows and scientific data management. First, it helps scientists to share processing pipelines implemented as workflows. Developing these processing pipelines and tools often is a recursive process

1. Introduction

of first finding tools developed by other scientists in the same domain, integrating them in a workflow and finally sharing the newly developed processing pipelines & tools by making them available as services to other scientists. Sharing services is a new form of scientific communication. Methods, algorithms used to be shared between scientists by means of publishing them in scientific journals. By implementing and publishing them as services they can be shared remotely and directly. To allow for this, we build the infrastructure to make scientific workflows available as services [50, 51].

Second, it addresses the problem of providing scientists with the infrastructure to host and execute the workflows. Maintaining and configuring workflow execution tools is difficult, particularly when running heterogeneous workflows and publishing them as services. Doing so leads to a continuously changing composite workload which cannot be serviced with just one static configuration. Clearly, scientists do not want to configure and repeatedly reconfigure the infrastructure to execute these workflows optimally themselves and we have therefore built fault-tolerant, self-configuring infrastructure that allows scalable execution of heterogeneous workflows [48, 49, 93].

Third, we address the problem of tracking the data lineage obtained from workflow executions. Data lineage tracking is important not only for understanding the origin of the data but also in order to be able to reproduce the data. In traditional experiments data lineage, i.e., what transformations were applied to what data, used to be recorded in a lab journal. Given the enormous amounts of data processed with such processing pipelines and their complexity manually tracking the lineage is no longer possible. Given the amount of lineage information captured from such experiments efficient methods for its storage must be found. For this we discuss the infrastructure needed to automatically and efficiently store what tools and what data have been used to derive data products [47].

The book is accordingly organized in three parts. The first part addresses the problem of how to publish scientific workflows as services. For this workflows need to be provided with proper interfaces enabling them to be called remotely and be recursively integrated in other workflows, applications and portals. To address this problem, we define how workflows can be efficiently published as stateful services by mapping the persistent state of the workflow executions to standard compliant interfaces as defined by the Web Services Resource Framework (WS-RF). Mapping workflows to WS-RF gives workflows a standardized interface that simplifies their reusability as well as integration and in the context of scientific workflows importantly, it enables management, monitoring, steering and adaptation of them.

The second part of this book describes the infrastructure for scalable workflow execution. Scientific workflows often orchestrate computationally intense tools and programs. To enable scalability for such workflows, they must be executed in a cluster. Although many distributed workflow engines exist, in practice, it remains a difficult problem to deploy such systems in an optimal configuration. In case such workflows are offered as a service, the system will face an unpredictable workload with high variability and manual reconfiguration is not an option. For this reason we designed an autonomic controller and implemented it for a workflow execution engine. Thanks to its autonomic controller, the engine features self-configuration, self-tuning and self-healing properties.

1. Introduction

The autonomic controller monitors the performance of the engine running on a cluster of computers and responds to workload variations by altering the configuration. In case failures occur, the controller can recover the workflow execution state from persistent storage and migrate it to a different node of the cluster. Such interventions are carried out without any human supervision. The autonomic controller can be configured using different autonomic control policies in order to work toward different goals. These policies remove the need for configuring the distributed execution engine but need to be configured themselves. We have developed several such policies gradually removing any need for manual configuration also of the policy itself. We have been able to demonstrate the feasibility and benefits of adding an autonomic controller to a distributed workflow execution engine with measurements for scientific as well as business workflows.

The third part of the book presents our approach to data lineage tracking in scientific workflows. Data lineage and data provenance have been identified as key problems in the management of scientific data. Not knowing the exact provenance and processing pipeline used to produce a derived data set often renders it useless from a scientific point of view. While capturing the data has been made simpler by workflow tools for processing scientific data, the problem of efficiently storing and querying such information has until now proven to be difficult as current solutions do not scale well. We have developed and implemented an algorithm to encode the lineage information, represented as a directed acyclic graph, and store it in a relational database. The approach allows for very efficient retrieval and querying of lineage information, significantly faster than known approaches. To do so, the approach uses a space and query efficient interval representation. Not all graphs can be encoded with it per se and so the main contribution of the new approach lies in transforming arbitrary lineage DAGs into graphs that can be stored using such representation. The approach performs well even for very large graphs representing very fine-grained lineage information.

Part I.

Workflow As A Service

2. Introduction

2.1. Introduction

The idea of process-based Web service composition and more recently process-based Grid service composition has gained widespread acceptance (e.g., [20, 64, 69]). Using workflows, already deployed services can be reused to build complex service compositions at a high level of abstraction. However, one important open issue that still needs more attention concerns the reusability of such compositions.

Workflows can be used to describe ad-hoc computations involving a well-defined set of services that are integrated to perform a certain computation once. They can then be generalized by making them parametric, in order for the same service composition to be reused with different input data sets. Furthermore, the same workflows can be bound to different service providers, allowing for the same algorithm structure (i.e., the workflow) to be reused with different building blocks (i.e., the services)[92]. Another interesting option – the focus of this part of the book – consists of reusing a service composition by publishing it as stateful service, making it available for integration into other workflows, applications or portals.

In this part of the book we discuss how to provide stateful computations with a standardized interface [38] simplifying their reusability and integration into applications, clients and portals. Giving workflows such a standardized and well-understood interface enables their management, monitoring, steering and adaptation. For this purpose we propose to map a workflow composing services to a service interface compliant with the Web Services Resource Framework and Web Services Notification set of specifications (WS-RF [30] and WS-N [83]). A workflow published as a Grid service can be accessed as a resource through a Web service interface, the WS-Resource, which provides standardized operations. The interface includes support for advanced functionality not found in stateless Web services, such as lifecycle management, property manipulation and event notification.

One important contribution of the work presented in this book lies in the definition of a precise mapping between the WS-RF concept of a resource and the persistent state of a service composition. Furthermore, our approach is general and can be used with process-based compositions defined using different modeling languages.

The mapping can be outlined as follows [51]. Lifecycle management of the resource provides a simplified way to manage the persistent state of the corresponding workflow execution. When the lifetime of the associated resource expires, the state can be garbage collected by the underlying process management system. Resource property manipulations are directly mapped to the state of the corresponding process instance, so that

2. Introduction

clients can for instance access intermediate results during the execution of the service composition and, to some extent, steer and control the computation by setting the values of the properties of the associated resource. Notifications can be used to inform clients about state changes, giving a powerful and efficient mechanism to report the progress of the execution of a workflow. Finally, the WS-RF concept of service groups can be used to manage batches of related process instances.

While such an interface for persistent computations greatly simplifies its integration by providing enhanced managing as well as monitoring capabilities, the performance overhead introduced by such a mapping is critical if it is supposed to scale for a large number of clients and resources. Thus, we need efficient mechanisms to create (i.e., start computations) and destroy resources, to read and write the state of the resource as well as to manage notifications and subscriptions, i.e., to match events with subscriptions and to send notifications.

We have implemented a layer on top of the JOpera workflow execution engine [93] providing workflows with such a WS-RF interface and present an extensive performance evaluation of the system scalability and overhead. This approach uses WS-Core (part of the Globus Toolkit [36]) to mirror the state of the execution of a workflow into a locally managed resource residing in the newly added layer. Mirroring all state in this layer however is not particularly efficient and the resulting system does not scale well when facing large numbers of client requests.

We therefore present an alternative implementation of the WS-RF and WS-N mapping for workflow systems which maps requests directly to operations of the workflow engine, thereby avoids maintaining mirrored state and thus provides improved scalability when servicing a large set of concurrent clients [50]. This approach embeds the state of the resource into the workflow execution engine by mapping the WS-RF requests to the engine's API. Although the first approach lets clients read resource property values faster, the performance of this mirrored architecture is limited due to the redundancies shared between the WS-RF layer and the underlying workflow engine. The second solution, mapping requests rather than mirroring resources, removes unnecessary layers of indirection and scales significantly better. To demonstrate this, we include an extensive performance comparison of the two approaches.

The remainder of this part is therefore structured as follows. The rest of this chapter discusses related work. In Chapter 3 we briefly present the WS-RF and WS-N standards, demonstrate how to map them to workflows and discuss the applications of it, i.e., what capabilities this gives clients integrating a workflow with such interface. We present the first implementation mirroring the state of the workflows in a layer on top the workflow execution engine and a first evaluation in Chapter 4. However as we show subsequently, the mirrored architecture does not scale well. The remainder of the chapter therefore discusses an alternative architecture which maps requests to the API of the engine and avoids the costly mirroring of the workflows. We compare the two approaches quantitatively in the same chapter. In Chapter 5 we draw conclusions.

2.2. Related Work

Only few research results are available in the context of turning applications or service compositions into services with a standardized stateful interface. Initial work [37] was concerned with providing distributed applications with a Web service interface. The interface was mainly used to authenticate and authorize users as well as instantiate applications. Similar work [41] was carried out in order to wrap command line-tools in Web services to make them available for remote users. The limitations of wrapping stateful resources with stateless Web services however have been well-understood in the meantime [29]. In [97] the authors describe a system which turns scientific legacy applications into Grid services and publishes these in a Grid portal. To do so a generic application independent WS-RF layer is added on top of the legacy application without having to generate additional code. This approach is similar to ours insofar as it provides applications with a stateful and standardized interface. Their implementation of the WS-RF layer does however not exploit the full potential of the WS-RF specifications by only implementing a small subset of the operations specified in WS-RF, thereby lacking the support for lifetime, property and notification management.

In addition to the approach presented in this book, there are currently five more implementations covering the entire WS-RF and WS-N standards. They differ mostly in the programming model as well as the implementation language. The most prominent implementation is the Java version of WS-Core which we used to implement the mirrored architecture and is distributed with the Globus Toolkit [36]. This code is also used in the two Apache projects Hermes (WS-N) and Apollo (WS-RF). An additional implementation of the standards which is part of the Globus Toolkit is implemented in C and lets one develop Grid services in C. pyGridWare [1] is also part of the Globus Toolkit. It allows the user to rapidly develop Grid services in Python. Similarly, WSRF.NET [56] is used to develop Grid services in any .NET language. With this implementation developing Grid services is not much different than programming Web services: the developer only needs to annotate what parts of the service should be made persistent. Lastly there is also a Perl implementation of the standards called WSRF::Lite [2].

These five implementations have been compared in terms of functionality and performance in [55]. This comparison however only focused on evaluating the performance of a single client setup (both, distributed on two machines and co-located). In our experiments we have used a setup with a large number of clients thereby showing how the system copes with a larger number of concurrent requests.

3. An Interface for Stateful Computations

Before discussing how to provide stateful computations modeled as workflows with a standardized interface, we first state the assumptions made about the workflow model in Section 3.1. The workflow model is generic and shared among many different workflow engines, therefore not restricting the application of our ideas. We then move on to explain how we model computations with workflows and do so by discussing the WS-RF & WS-N standards and how we map them to workflows in Section 3.2. In Section 3.3 we discuss the applications of such a mapping, i.e. how the mapping allows a client to execute, manage, monitor and steer workflows.

3.1. Workflow Model

In this section we state our assumptions about how workflows are used to model computations composed of any type of service. We also define the persistent state associated with such computations as well as their lifecycle, so that it becomes clear what information should be provided by a workflow management infrastructure in order for our approach to be applicable.

The concept of workflow is shared among several scientific workflow languages and tools like GSFL [64], Pegasus [31], AGWL [35], Triana [109], ScyFlow [74], GridFlow [19], JOpera [90], xWFE [125] and Karajan [119].

A workflow is a composition of tasks connected by data flow and control flow. Workflows also have input parameters, holding the data passed to the workflow, and output parameters storing the results of the computation. Tasks (equivalent to jobs in ScyFlow and activities in BPEL, AGWL and GSFL) refer mostly to Grid services which also have input and output parameters associated with them. The data passed to a service is copied into the input parameters whereas the results coming from a service invocation are copied into the output parameters of the task. The data flow defines how the results of a service invocation are copied into the input parameters of the next tasks. The control flow defines the order of invocation of the distinct service invocations. Neither Karajan or xWFE explicitly distinguish between control flow and data flow, but instead derive the control flow from the data flow dependencies. This, however, does not hinder the applicability of our approach. In fact, when we define the mapping between a workflow and a resource we are mostly interested in its runtime execution state.

The runtime state of a workflow can be defined to be all data associated with its execution. Since the same workflow can be executed multiple times, such state is typically structured in several instances that can be active concurrently. Each instance stores a set of state attributes comprising the values of the input and output parameters (referred to as input/output data set in GridFlow, variables in BPEL, data packages in AGWL, parameters in xWFL and input/output files in Karajan) of all its service invocations including the workflow itself, as well as workflow and task attributes written by the execution engine. These attributes include meta-data such as execution times of tasks and workflows determined by the execution engine, the current execution status of tasks and workflows (e.g., waiting, running, finished, failed, etc.) and other execution related information which may differ depending on the engine.

The lifecycle of a workflow instance begins when a workflow is instantiated. During the execution of the instance, its state will be accumulated and stored persistently. This implies that all intermediate results, i.e., results of task invocations, remain available after the task has finished and the following tasks have consumed them. The final results will also be saved once the computation is finished. At the end of the lifecycle of a workflow instance, its state will be removed from the persistent storage. It is worth noting that the end of the lifecycle of the instance and the end of the computation do not necessarily coincide: after the instance has finished executing, the state will still be available, allowing the history of the computation to be read from persistent storage (see part III of this book).

3.2. Mapping Workflows to WS-Resources

The specifications that constitute the Web Service Resource Framework have been defined in order to shift from the stateless paradigm of plain Web services to the stateful model of Grid services [29].

To do so, WS-RF [43] loosely couples a Web service with a stateful resource and provides well-defined methods to monitor and manage its state In this context, a Web service that provides a standardized set of operations to access the state of the resource associated with it is called a WS-Resource. The areas of standardized operations span lifecycle management, property manipulation and service groups as specified in WS-ResourceLifetime [45], WS-ResourceProperties [45] and WS-ServiceGroup [73] respectively. In order to also provide publish-subscribe interaction patterns for Web services, the WS-N set of specifications (WS-BaseNotification [44] and WS-Topics [115]) has been brought forward.

Together, the WS-N and WS-RF set of specifications define the Grid service interface [29]. In the following we give a brief outline of the specifications and also provide a detailed mapping of the specified operations to the persistent state of a stateful computation defined as a workflow.

3.2.1. WS-Resource

This specification defines the implied resource pattern [30] as being the relationship between a Web service, the WS-resource, and a resource. A WS-Resource is defined to be a Web service through which clients can access the state of a resource and manage its lifetime. The WS-Resource uses implementation specific means to access the underlying resource. The specification is not very restrictive with respect to what can be considered a resource. The only requirements a resource has to satisfy is that it needs to be uniquely identifiable and that it has properties. Workflow instances meet these requirements as they are usually associated with unique identifiers and contain state information which can be interpreted as properties.

Thus, we propose to map a workflow instance storing the state of the execution of a composite service to a resource. As we are going to show, clients can manage a workflow instance through the standard operations provided by a WS-Resource interface. Because the set of state attributes (i.e., the properties) is identical for all instances of a given workflow, only one WS-Resource interface per workflow is required to operate on all instances of the particular workflow. However, for each workflow that is published as a stateful service, an additional WS-Resource interface is required.

Furthermore, since the mapping between resources and workflow instances is a bijection and each workflow instance already has its own unique identifier, we can reuse the same identifier for the corresponding resource. Thus, the workflow identifier becomes part of the resource endpoint reference and will have to be included in all messages sent to the WS-Resource in order to correlate the client request with the individual workflow instance.

3.2.2. WS-ResourceLifetime

The WS-ResourceLifetime specification defines the management of a resource by providing means to either destroy a resource instance immediately via the **Destroy** operation or to schedule its destruction at a specific point in time by using the **SetTerminationTime** operation. The scheduled destruction time is a property of the WS-Resource and can therefore be queried, set and thereby extended accordingly.

Both operations defined in this specification, immediate and scheduled destruction, are mapped to the lifecycle of the workflow instance and its state. In addition to discarding the state of a workflow instance, destruction will also interrupt and terminate the ongoing execution (if the workflow is still running).

Since the specification does not include a standard mechanism for resource creation, we discuss several alternatives for instantiating a new workflow upon resource creation. Related to this, we also describe two additional operations to control the state of the workflow associated with a resource, once it has been created.

The first way to create a resource, is through the **startProcess** operation. This operation instantiates a workflow and begins its execution after having allocated a new resource for it. In some cases, e.g., for parameter sweep computations [3], the same workflow is started multiple times with different input parameter values. Calling the **startProcess** operation several times to do so may be expensive. Thus, we also provide the **startBatch** operation which, instead of starting only one workflow, starts a batch of identical workflows that may receive different input data.

Additionally, in order to enable more fine-grained lifecycle management of the workflow execution we provide the (non-standard) **Suspend** and **Resume** operations which allow the client to pause the execution of a workflow and to subsequently resume it. The suspend operation amounts to setting a breakpoint before the next task which is to be executed. Execution will be suspended once the breakpoint is reached. These two operations can be used in conjunction with the ability of modifying property values of the associated resource, so that the changes can be applied by assuring the client that the state of the suspended workflow has not changed and thus ensuring the consistency of the result.

Finally, the **startSuspended** operation is an atomic combination of the **startProcess** and **Suspend** operation which prepares a new workflow instance for execution but does not start it. This operation can for instance be useful to start a workflow, subscribe to its topics and only then resume execution, thereby making sure none of the notifications sent due to the subscriptions is missed.

3.2.3. WS-ResourceProperties

This specification defines how the properties associated with the state of a resource can be accessed using a pull mechanism and how they can be modified. Published properties of a resource are defined in a document associated with the resource. A client can retrieve the properties document from a resource via the **GetResourcePropertyDocument** operation or can query the resource for specific properties by invoking the **QueryResourceProperties** operation and can read or write the values of these properties using the **GetResourceProperty** and **SetResourceProperty** operations respectively.

In the case of resources representing workflows, their properties can be directly mapped to the workflow execution state. Since the persistent state of a workflow can be modeled as a set of attributes as described in Section 3.1, each of these can be accessed by clients through the corresponding property of the resource. Thus, each input and output parameter of the workflow (and its tasks) as well as execution related meta-data (e.g., profiling, debugging, error handling information that is accumulated during the execution of the workflow) is mapped to a specific property. Given the data flow structure of a workflow, it is possible to automatically generate the corresponding resource's property document by enumerating its state attributes.

In particular, we distinguish between read-only and read-write properties. There is no need to be able to write properties mapped to intermediate results of tasks as well as to final results of the workflow (i.e., mapped to output parameters). Also, writing properties that are mapped to instance attributes set by the execution engine should not be allowed. In fact, doing so would invalidate the state of the workflow. Additionally, there are also constraints regarding the time when such properties can be read. That is, they can only be read after having been initialized by the execution engine. Violating these rules leads to a fault message sent to the client.

In contrast to the read-only properties there is also a set of read-write properties. Input parameters to tasks and also the workflow are defined to be read-write properties.

However, also in this case there is no need to be able to write to properties that map to input parameters that have already been used for the computation since it will not have any influence on the workflow execution. Writing such a property will therefore also lead to a fault message.

3.2.4. WS-ServiceGroup

With this specification, groups are used as a classification mechanism to simplify the discovery and management of sets of WS-Resources. WS-Resources are not allowed to freely join groups, but must meet certain criteria defined for each group. Groups can then in turn be queried to find all members.

We map the concepts defined in the WS-ServiceGroup specification to the execution of batches of related workflows. To do so, service groups are defined so that membership is restricted to only allow resources representing workflow instances belonging to the same execution batch to join the group.

3.2.5. WS-BaseNotification / WS-Topics

The WS-BaseNotification and WS-Topics specifications define the push mechanism used by clients to be informed about changes occurring at the resource. With these, clients are notified using an asynchronous event-notification interaction pattern. A client can subscribe to topics defined by a WS-Resource using the **Subscribe** operation and will receive the corresponding notifications from it. The various topics provided by a resource are defined as one of its resource properties and can thus be queried for.

Similar to the resource properties, we define the attributes of the state of a workflow instance to be available as topics. This means that whenever a state attribute changes, subscribed clients will receive a notification. The notification sent to the clients also includes the new value of the attribute, in order to reduce the load on the WS-Resource server.

As an extension, we also include the **startSubscribed** operation, which atomically instantiates a resource and subscribes to its changes (the topic is passed as a parameter). This way, clients are guaranteed not to lose notification messages.

3.3. Applications

In this section we discuss how the previously described mapping improves the handling of persistent computations in the areas of lifecycle management, monitoring, and steering of one or a batch of workflows.

3.3.1. Lifecycle Management

Mapping WS-Lifetime to the lifecycle of workflows and their state provides a useful and elegant technique to deal with the problem of managing the accumulated state of past executions of a workflow. This allows clients to define during what time frame they are interested in the computation's results to remain stored persistently. If the computation terminates within this window, its results will be kept as part of its persistent state as long as the resource instance is not destroyed. Otherwise, the computation will be aborted upon the expiration of the corresponding resource's lifetime and its state will be discarded at a well-defined and predictable time. This is an improvement with respect to other systems that resort to manual ad-hoc techniques to manage the results of past computations (e.g., [67]).

3.3.2. Monitoring and Steering

Using property manipulation a client is able to read and write properties that map to attributes of the underlying state. More specifically, by reading properties a client can poll for the current state. Thus, a resource can be queried to find out what task has been reached by the workflow, to retrieve intermediate results or to download the final results once the workflow execution has completed. However, if a client requires to be informed about a change of a state attribute mapped to a property, with this property-based mechanism it still needs to periodically poll the resource to find out about the new value. An alternative method to monitor the workflow and its execution is thus provided by the topics to which the client can subscribe and about which it will receive a notification once the value of the corresponding property changes. This subscribe/notify form of interaction enables a push model relieving the client from having to poll for the changed value and the service provider from the overhead introduced by polling clients. A client can subscribe to execution state changes of individual tasks of the workflow and is thereby able to track the progress of the workflow execution.

Steering of workflows can be achieved by proactively setting properties to different values. With this, for instance, a client becomes able to reset the value of an input parameter of a task depending on the result or the value of an output parameter of a different task. Thus, it can steer the execution by following different paths in the control flow and adapting the data flow of the running workflow. Since partial results are sent to the client through notifications, a client can use this information to perform a form of error recovery: if results indicate that an exception or failure has occurred, the client can take corrective actions and reset input parameters of tasks yet to be executed. To do so in a safe way in order to avoid inconsistencies, the client should suspend the execution of the workflow by interactively setting a breakpoint on a specific task or by pausing the execution of the entire workflow immediately. The client is informed with a notification when the breakpoint is reached. After the values of the selected properties have been corrected, the client can resume execution (**Resume**).

3.3.3. Managing workflow batches

We use the concept of service groups to manage workflow batches. With this, a client can add all started workflows belonging to a batch to a service group. Clients can then read the properties of the service group to find all workflow instances of the batch. Using

3. An Interface for Stateful Computations

the concept of the service group in this context therefore provides a convenient way of grouping workflow instances so that they can be managed and monitored as a whole. For example, workflows can be grouped by a caller-callee relationship, so that the state of a set of nested workflows is treated as a single resource. This in turn can be used to keep track of the execution of the entire set of workflows and to garbage collect multiple (but related) workflow instances when the corresponding resource is destroyed.

4. Design

In this chapter we discuss alternative implementations of the previously presented mapping. In Section 4.1 we first briefly describe the workflow engine which we have extended. We then discuss a first approach for the implementation in Section 4.2 and evaluate it. As we can demonstrate with the measurements, the first implementation faces significant scalability issues. We therefore present a second approach in Section 4.3 and compare both approaches in Section 4.4.

4.1. JOpera Workflow Execution Engine

In this section we provide a high level description of a workflow engine architecture. We do so in order to describe the constraints imposed by the architecture of Grid workflow engines and to illustrate the mapping between workflows and WS-RF/WS-N compliant services, i.e., Grid services. We take JOpera [88] as an example.

4.1.1. Workflow Design and Execution

Using JOpera, developers compose Grid services into workflows which are then automatically published as Grid services. The workflows are visually composed out of different heterogeneous tasks (mixing coarse grained Grid and Web service invocations with fine grained Java snippets) which are linked by a control flow and a data flow graph [90]. The control flow defines the partial order of invocation of the tasks while the data flow is a directed graph which defines the data to be copied between the tasks, i.e., what data is copied between output and input parameters of tasks.

For each execution, a new instance of a workflow is created. The runtime state of a workflow instance consists of all data associated with the execution. This includes all the values of the input and output parameters of the tasks and the workflow, as well as process and task attributes written by the execution engine (e.g., execution status, debugging, profiling and lineage tracking information, and other execution related metadata). The state of the computation can be stored persistently in a database.

4.1.2. Execution Engine Architecture

The JOpera workflow execution includes of following components (Figure 4.1).

Execution Engine API: The JOpera execution engine provides an API for clients to issue commands and interact with the engine and the workflows deployed therein. Once a workflow is deployed, a client can request to start it. To do so, the engine instantiates the workflow and begins with the execution. The API provides clients with the ability to start, to stop and to manage workflows and their instances.

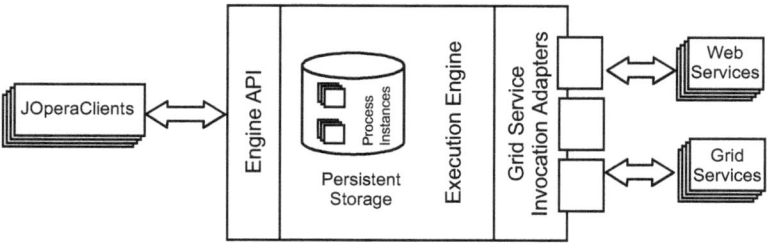

Figure 4.1.: Architecture of the JOpera workflow execution engine

Execution Engine: The execution engine is in charge of executing workflow instances. It follows the control flow to determine what tasks to execute and the data flow for moving data between tasks. The tasks are executed through the service invocation adapters. For each workflow instance the engine stores intermediate and final results in the persistent storage.

Service Invocation Adapters: The engine dispatches task executions to the Grid service adapters. These adapters carry out the actual invocation of the Grid service. The execution engine can use different adapters for different kinds of services.

4.2. Mirrored Architecture

In this section we describe a first implementation of the mapping of workflows to resources using the WS-Core implementation of WS-RF and WS-N. WS-Core provides a complete implementation of the WS-RF and WS-N specifications [55]. Being written in Java, it can easily be integrated with the JOpera engine. At the end of this section we evaluate the approach and motivate the need for a more lightweight implementation.

4.2.1. Architecture

The mirrored architecture (Figure 4.2, left) builds on the idea of using the WS-Core implementation and to follow its programming model. This prescribes to develop a Web Service, the WS-Resource, as well as a resource. Web service and resource are linked by the *ResourceHome* which is used to create, find, manage and potentially persist resources. Following this model, we have mapped JOpera workflows into resources, developed the necessary WS-Resource and used the *ResourceHome* accordingly. With

4. Design

this, the state of the resource (located in the WS-Core hosting environment) reflects the state of the corresponding workflow instance (located inside the underlying Grid workflow engine).

Furthermore, only one WS-Resource needs to be deployed for each workflow. This interface provides access to all of its resource instances as they are addressed by the endpoint reference sent along with each client request.

In the following, we present how each part of the standardized interface has been implemented in this mirrored architecture.

Lifecycle management

When receiving a client request to instantiate a workflow, the WS-Resource will first create a resource in the hosting environment. Doing so will trigger the resource to also create a workflow instance in the underlying execution engine using the engine's API. Since resource instance and workflow instance are tightly coupled, the resource instance is identified by the workflow instance identifier, which is returned by the WS-Resource to the client.

Should a client request the immediate termination of a workflow instance, the WS-Resource will destroy its resource instance which in turn destroys the workflow instance. In case of a scheduled destruction, this implementation relies on the mechanisms provided by WS-Core to destroy the resource instance in due time. Also in this case, destruction of the resource instance will lead to the destruction of the workflow instance.

Properties

The WS-Resource provides clients with access to the workflow instance properties. To do so, the WS-Resource maintains a list of all properties that can be read and written by clients. This list is the same for all instances of a workflow and can therefore be defined when the workflow is deployed. A resource instance maintains a copy of all properties and synchronizes each of these with the properties of the workflow instance. This is very efficient for read operations where the value need not be read from the workflow instance but can be returned immediately upon request. If, however, the value of a state element of a workflow instance changes, this method incurs the overhead of having to update the cached property value in the resource instance. Similarly, changes of resource properties triggered by clients (e.g., through a set property operation) need to be forwarded to the underlying engine's API.

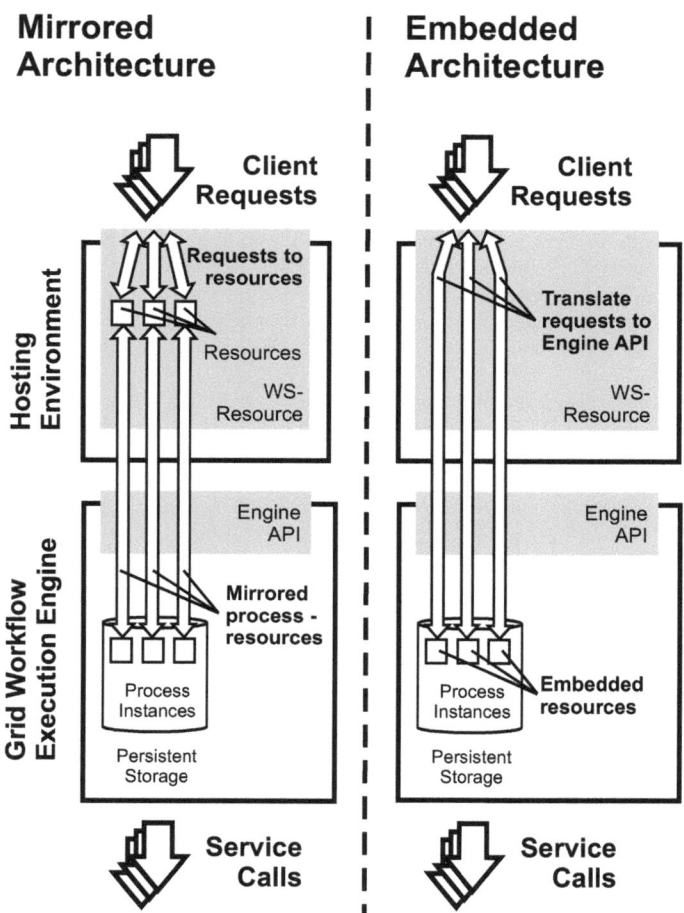

Figure 4.2.: Mirrored Architecture (left) discussed in Section 4.2 and Embedded Architecture (right) presented in Section 4.3

4. Design

Notifications

As mentioned earlier, the topics to which clients can subscribe are the elements of the execution state of a workflow instance. Once a client is subscribed to a particular topic, it will receive a notification once the value of the corresponding workflow state element changes.

In order to send out notifications, the resource instance registers listeners with the engine for the property values the clients have subscribed to. When the value of a topic changes, the engine calls back the resource instance and informs it about the change. The resource instance will then notify the WS-Resource which in turn will send out notification messages to subscribed clients.

4.2.2. Evaluation

In this section we evaluate the performance of the WS-RF enabled workflow execution engine. We focus on determining the cost of several resource creation alternatives and showing that the system can to handle a very large number of resources. However, as we show, the system does not scale well in face of a large number of clients accessing the service simultaneously, motivating the work presented in the following section.

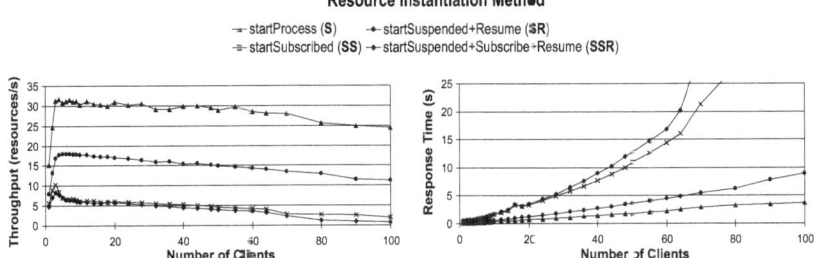

Figure 4.3.: Throughput and response time of different resource instantiation methods

The experiments have been carried out by installing the JOpera Grid service composition engine on a server running Linux (RedHat AS 4), equipped with two AMD Opteron 2.4GHz CPUs and 2GB of memory. The clients were running on a cluster of 64 dual processor (1Ghz) nodes connected with a 100Mb/s local area network.

Resource Creation

In a first set of experiments, we measured the time required to instantiate a workflow and to subscribe to one of its properties in 4 different ways. We did the first using the **startProcess (S)** and the combination of **startSuspended** and **Resume (SR)**. The latter was done with a combination of the three operations **startSuspended**, **Subscribe** and **Resume** (**SSR**) and also with these three operations merged into one, the **startSubscribed** (**SS**) operation. We ran the experiments with up to 100 concurrent clients. The response time and the throughput are shown in Figure 4.3.clients ranging from 1 to 100, each requesting the creation of 100 resources. The results are shown in Figure 4.3 with the response time at the top and the throughput at the bottom of the figure.

Response Time: Resource creation with **S** has a lower response time than **SR** because in the former case only one operation is invoked compared to two in the latter case. The response time for instantiation requests in both cases scales linearly with the number of clients. Also **SS** performs faster than **SSR**. This can again be attributed to the fact that the former is executing only one operation whereas the latter executes three. From the results it can also be observed that the operations involving a subscription (**SS** and **SSR**) are significantly slower than the others, even in the case of **SS**, where instantiation and subscription are done atomically. Thus, the time required to subscribe to a topic outweighs the time required for message transfer.

Throughput: The throughput (Figure 4.3 bottom) for the different methods of resource creation gives a similar picture as the response time: **S** has the highest throughput, followed by **SR**. Again, the two methods that include a subscription to a topic, **SS** and **SSR**, have the lowest throughput. This shows that subscription is costly, as multiple concurrent clients must be synchronized to access the shared resources subscription table. This operation gets slower the more resources are present. For the operations involving a subscription, we have also measured the throughput of the notifications sent by the Grid service container to the clients, observing that at most 26 notifications/second could be sent for 6 clients, each creating and subscribing to 100 resources.

Workflow batch instantiation: In order to motivate the need for the **startBatch** operation, we have also compared the time it takes to instantiate workflow batches of different sizes by calling the **startProcess** operation repeatedly and the **startBatch** operation once. As can be seen in Figure 4.4, starting the workflow batch with the **startBatch** operation is drastically faster. With it, creating 10^5 resources takes less than a second, compared to almost 3 hours with the **startProcess** operation.

Querying Properties Overhead

In this experiment we used one client to create a resource and get the value of one of its properties and measured the time it requires to execute the **getResourceProperty** operation. The results shown in Figure 4.5 indicate that the time required for the operation increases linearly with the number of resources instantiated starting at 40ms and growing to only 70ms when 100'000 resources have been created. This is because before the value of the property can be read and be sent back, also here the resource must be found first. The process of finding a resource of course takes longer with an increasing number of instantiated resources.

4. Design

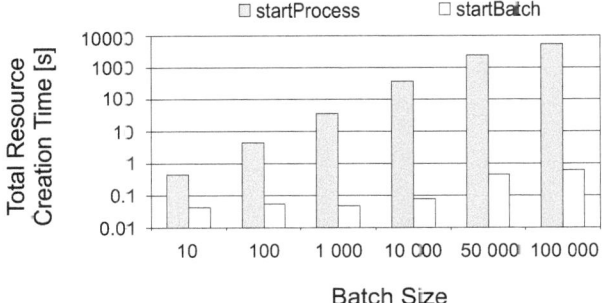

Figure 4.4.: Comparison of different methods for starting workflow batches

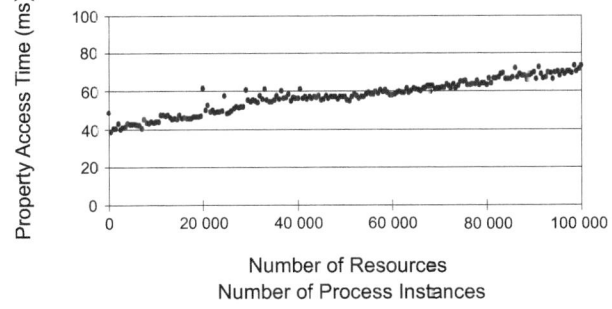

Figure 4.5.: Property access overhead with an increasingly large number of resources

Scalability

The goal of this experiment is to perform a basic evaluation of the scalability of the mirrored architecture and to study the design problems that limit it. For these measurements we have used the same set up as before. Up to two clients were run on each node. In order to reduce the size of the configuration space, the WS-Core installation was configured to use a pool of 100 threads to handle client requests and all security mechanisms were disabled.

First, we measured the throughput of the raw hosting environment. By deploying a simple Web service and invoking it with up to 100 concurrent clients, we observed that this amount of clients is not enough to saturate the Web service (Figure 4.6). Unfortunately, this result does not hold for the WS-Resource used to create resources by calling the Grid workflow engine. For this case, our results indicate that the throughput reaches the maximum at 36 resource creations per second with only 5 clients. Clearly, this performance is not enough in large scale applications.

In order to find the bottleneck, we have analyzed the execution profile of resource creation requests. WS-Core builds on its own hosting environment. Client requests are

4. Design

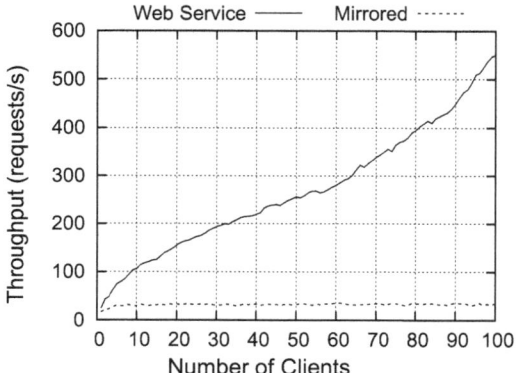

Figure 4.6.: Comparison of the throughput when calling a raw Web service and the create resource operation of the WS-Resource

accepted by a *ServiceDispatcher* which uses a pool of *ServiceThread*s to service them. In our experiments, this pool was configured to use up to 100 threads, therefore we believe that the scalability problem is not due to a misconfiguration of the system. Moreover, as the throughput of the plain Web service indicates, the loss in performance happens past this point.

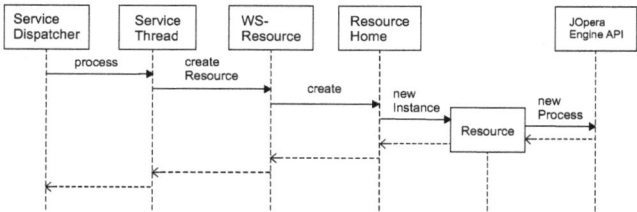

Figure 4.7.: Sequence diagram of the resource creation operation

Following the profile shown in Figure 4.7, a *ServiceThread* locates the deployed Web service (in our case the WS-Resource) and calls it to execute the requested operation on the resource. To do so, first the resource object is located (or created), one of its methods is called and the results are returned to the client. In this architecture, resources are managed by a central component, the *ResourceHome*. Thus, when a resource is created, the WS-Resource delegates this operation to the *ResourceHome*, which instantiate a new *Resource* object. As part of the implementation of our mapping, the constructor of the *Resource* class instantiates a workflow by calling the engine's API.

4. Design

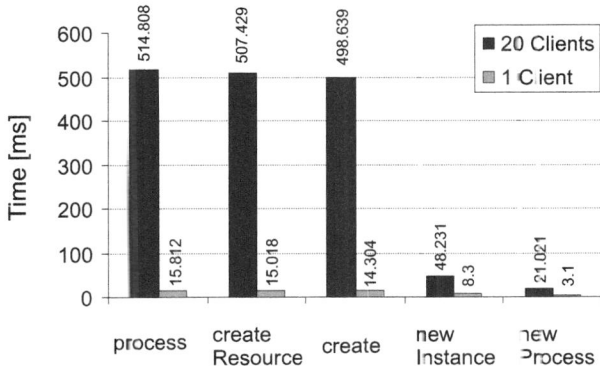

Figure 4.8.: Average time required for each of the methods called when creating a resource (as shown in Figure 4.7) in case of 1 and 20 client(s)

We measured the time needed for each of these steps in case of 1 client and 20 concurrent clients (Figure 4.8). The time spent in the *create* method is much bigger than the time actually required for instantiating the resource in case of 20 clients. The relative difference between these two times is not as big in case only one client is creating resources. This clearly indicates a contention problem in the *create* method preventing multiple clients from creating resources simultaneously.

From this analysis it can be concluded that while linking the WS-Resource and the resources using the *ResourceHome* adds flexibility (in terms of finding, managing and making resources persistent), it also involves synchronized access to the resources. This synchronization is thus the main reason for the increased time required to create resources when multiple clients are doing so concurrently. This bottleneck leads to the performance loss observed in Figure 4.6.

4.3. Embedded Architecture

As shown in the previous section, synchronized access to the *ResourceHome* can amount to a performance penalty when a large number of clients accesses a resource simultaneously.

In the context of publishing workflows as resources, the mechanisms provided by the *ResourceHome* are not strictly needed. Equivalent functionality to the one provided by the *ResourceHome* is available in the vast majority of Grid workflow engines. As a consequence, the API of the engine can be directly used to find, manage, destroy and create the workflow instances. In this architecture, the WS-Resource only provides a translation of all client requests in terms of the engine API. This way, the state of the resources becomes embedded into the engine. Although this involves accessing the engine for all resource operations, it removes unnecessary redundancies and, as we are going to show, provides much better scalability.

Figure 4.2 (right) depicts the embedded architecture of the WS-RF specification implementation in the context of JOpera. Clients interact with the WS-Resource hosted on top of the execution engine API. The WS-Resource uses the API to access the resources stored in the persistent storage. Different workflows designed and run in JOpera are mapped to different WS-Resources. Still, there is only one WS-Resource made accessible in the hosting environment. This WS-Resource uses the URI to map the request to a given workflow and the endpoint in order to map it to a particular instance of the workflow.

Upon arrival of requests, the WS-Resource will directly use the engine's API to access the persistent storage in order to store and retrieve information about the state of instances. With this solution access to resources is synchronized on the lowest possible level: only read and write access to the same resource is synchronized by using thread-safe data structures.

4.3.1. Lifecycle management

When receiving a request to create a resource, the WS-Resource reads the workflow name out of the URI from the request received and instantiates a workflow. The identifier of the workflow is returned as the ID of the resource. Destruction, be it immediate or scheduled, removes the accumulated state of the workflow instance and if necessary also interrupts workflow execution.

4.3.2. Properties

Properties in the embedded implementation are handled as follows: when a client requests to read a property of a resource instance, the WS-Resource uses the engine API to retrieve the value from the persistent storage. In case of a write property request, the WS-Resource will also use the engine's API to write the value directly into the persistent storage.

4.3.3. Notifications

Subscriptions to topics are also considered to be resources according to the specification [44]. In the embedded implementation this would mean to map them to a workflow and to create a workflow instance every time a client subscribes. Subscriptions however do not require the flexibility provided by workflows and it is therefore more efficient and simpler to store them in a list located in the WS-Resource. To be able to send out notifications once changes in the state of the resource occur, we use a mechanism provided by the JOpera execution engine. The WS-Resource registers listeners with the engine and will receive notifications once state changes occur. It will then match subscriptions with the state changes and will send out the corresponding notifications.

4.4. Comparison

The goal of this second set of measurements is to show and compare the performance under heavy load induced by an increasing number of clients concurrently accessing a resource through the WS-Resource interface using the mirrored and the embedded architecture. The same setup that has been used for the initial measurements presented in Section 4.2.2 has also been used for these experiments.

4.4.1. WS-Resource Creation

Although resource creation is not specified in the WS-RF set of specifications, it remains a very important operation. In our case, it represents the submission of a new computation to be started by the workflow engine. In a first series of experiments we have therefore measured the response time and the throughput when a variable number of clients simultaneously initiates the execution of a workflow instance by creating the corresponding resource.

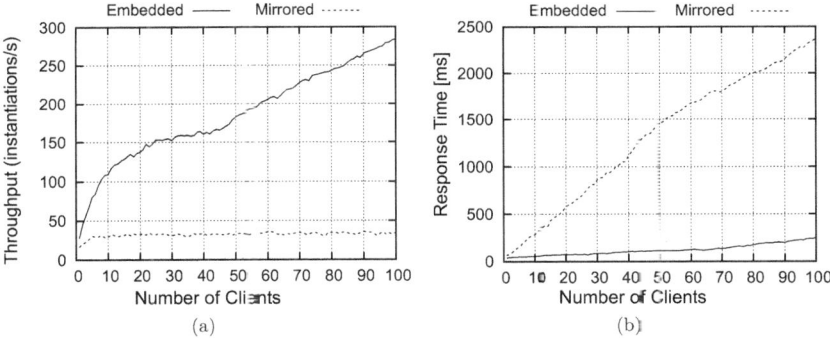

Figure 4.9.: Throughput (a) and response time (b) of the create resource operation

Figure 4.9(a) shows the number of resources created per second when using both architectures serving up to 100 clients at a time. Each client creates 1000 resources as fast as possible. The mirrored architecture reaches its peak throughput of 36 new resources/second with only 5 clients. We have investigated this problem and presented our findings in Section 4.2.2. The embedded architecture does not suffer from this limitation and it reaches a throughput of over 250 resources/second with 100 clients. In this case, we were not able to saturate the system.

Figure 4.9(b) shows the response times for resource creation. With an increasing number of clients concurrently creating resources, the response time increases as is to be expected. In case of the mirrored architecture, the response time grows very high, to up to 2.4s in case of 100 concurrent clients. This is because this implementation is only able to serve up to 36 clients requests per second while additional requests will have to wait. The response time in case of the embedded architecture grows one order of magnitude less (0.25s), as the system has enough capacity to deal with 100 clients.

4.4.2. WS-Properties

In these experiments an increasing number of clients reads the property of a single resource 1000 times. The response time for both architectures only grows slowly with an increasing number of clients (Figure 4.10(b)). The throughput increases linearly when more clients read the properties in case of both architectures. In this case, the mirrored architecture outperforms the embedded one. This can be explained by a caching effect. The state of the resource is kept closer to the clients and is thus faster to access. Given that all clients were reading from the same resource, the cache in the *ResourceHome* is able to fulfill all requests.

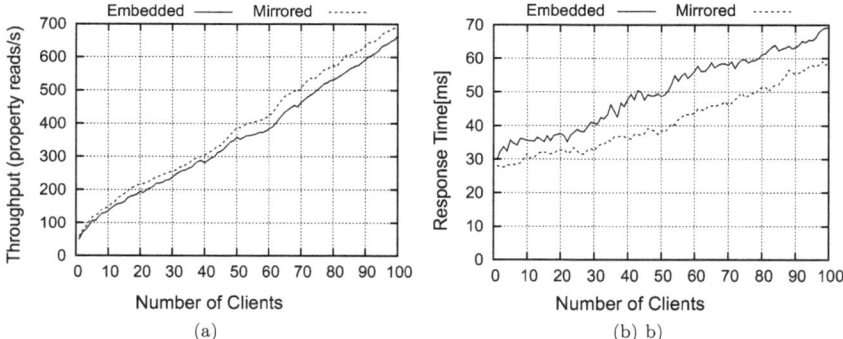

Figure 4.10.: Throughput (a) and response time (b) of the read property operation

In case of the embedded architecture, requests of reading property values have to be mapped to queries to the underlying engine API, which makes their execution path about 10ms longer with 100 concurrent clients. Nevertheless, this overhead seems acceptable in view of the advantages in other performance measurements.

4.4.3. WS-Notification

In a next series of experiments we have measured the different implementations of WS-Notification. In the first experiment we have measured the time it takes a client to subscribe to a certain topic. To do so, an increasing number of clients (1 to 100) subscribes to 1000 topics as fast as possible. We have measured the throughput and the response time for both architectures. In case of the mirrored architecture, we used two configurations of WS-Core. The first stores subscriptions in memory, the second one makes them persistent on disk.

The mirrored architecture relies on WS-Core to manage its subscriptions. WS-Core follows the WS-N specification and treats subscriptions as resources. Thus, it uses a *SubscriptionHome*, which inherits the scalability problems of the *ResourceHome* implementation. As our measurements indicate (Figure 4.11(a)), the throughput reaches a maximum at 50 subscriptions/second. As expected, persistent subscriptions are more expensive than volatile ones (Figure 4.11(b)).

As previously described, the embedded implementation relies on the engine's API to maintain the client subscriptions and only maps the WS-N topics to the addressing mechanism used by the engine to identify each element of a workflow execution state which may change. This greatly speeds up subscribing to a topic, as we observed from the throughput which grows linearly with the increasing number of concurrent subscribers.

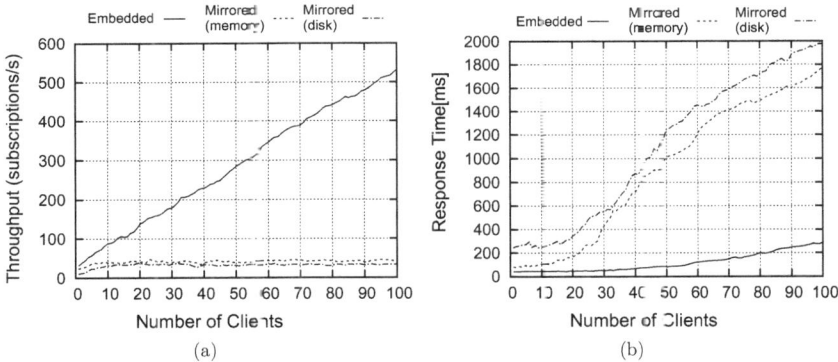

Figure 4.11.: Throughput (a) and response time (b) for the subscribe operation

In the next experiment we measured the throughput of the two architectures in terms of sending out notifications. Although there are many combinations of the number of subscribers, number of resources and number of subscriptions to topics that could affect this performance metric we focus on one setup. Each client (from 1 to 100) subscribes to one topic of the same shared resource. This resource goes through 100 state changes, which will be reported to all subscribed clients by sending them 100 notification messages. Thus, in the experiment, the Grid service sends from 100 notifications (with 1 client) up to 10'000 notifications (with 100 clients).

4. Design

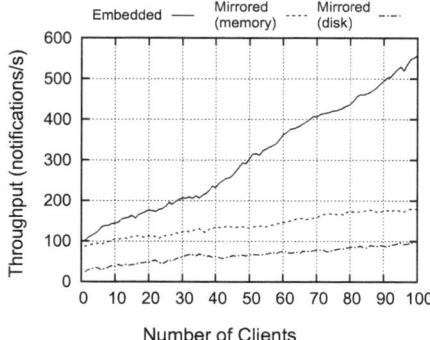

Figure 4.12.: Throughput for matching events with subscriptions and sending notifications

For both architectures, the throughput does not saturate with 100 clients. However, the mirrored architecture is only able to send 180 notifications/second (with volatile subscriptions) and 100 msg/s (persistent subscription). The embedded architecture sends out notifications at a higher rate (550 msg/s). The reason for this performance improvement lies in the fact that in the mirrored implementation the local copy of the state needs to be updated whenever a notification from the engine is received. Furthermore, this implementation relies on WS-Core to call back subscribed clients, and it appears that each notification is sent out sequentially. Instead, in case of the embedded architecture this is not a limitation as clients are notified in parallel.

5. Conclusions

In this part of the book we presented our approach to bridge the gap between two abstractions: resources and workflows. We did so in order to enable recursive composition of potentially stateful services, where the workflow defining how services are composed, is published itself as a stateful service. This mapping has been described in terms of the concepts defined by the Web Service Resource Framework (WS-RF) and Notifications (WS-N) and is applicable to several service composition languages and tools sharing the notion of a workflow or process. With it, stateful computations modeled with a workflow at design-time can be managed at run-time through a standardized interface provided by the corresponding resource. By reporting on the implementation of such a mapping, we have shown the feasibility of using a WS-Resource interface to initiate, monitor, steer, suspend, resume and delete the persistent execution state of a computation by creating and destroying the associated resource and reading, writing and subscribing to its properties.

We have first considered an architecture where this mapping is implemented by mirroring the persistent state of the execution of a workflow as the state of the published resource. This has the advantage, as our experimental results show, that clients can directly access such resources without the overhead of going through additional layers of the system. Furthermore, wrapping the API of a workflow engine within WS-Core also reduces the development effort required to make the workflow engine standard compliant, as the infrastructure providing the implementation of such standards can be reused. The disadvantage of this approach lies in the redundancy introduced in the system, where the state of the resources is duplicated across different components. This has the drawback that concurrency control is performed early in the request processing pipeline and the scalability of the system suffers when facing a large number of concurrent clients.

As an alternative, we have presented a second architecture, where the state of a resource is embedded into the underlying workflow engine and the mapping involves a direct translation of the client requests from the standardized WS-RF interface to the engine API. Although with this solution all requests have to be serviced through the engine, incurring in slightly higher response time, the embedded architecture scales much better as the concurrency control is performed on a more fine grained level within the workflow execution engine. The results of our experimental performance evaluation of the second approach indicate that the overhead introduced is minimal and that the system scales well to manage the lifecycle of hundreds of thousands of resources representing workflow instances in the underlying execution engine.

Part II.
Autonomic Workflow Execution

6. Introduction

6.1. Motivation

Workflow management systems are increasingly being applied to domains beyond traditional business process automation. Examples include e-commerce [98, 116], virtual laboratories [5], DNA sequencing [77], scientific computing [7, 75], and Grid computing [19]. More recently, the idea of process-based Web service composition [20, 69] as well as modeling and enforcing business conversations and protocols followed by Web services [6, 68, 126] has gained widespread acceptance.

Such open service oriented architectures face an important scalability problem when the services published on the Web become successful. Successful services have the potential to be concurrently invoked by a very large number of clients [84], imposing high demands on the underlying workflow management infrastructure. Whenever a new conversation is started, a new workflow instance has to be created. Then, for every message exchanged with the service, the state of the underlying workflow has to be updated to reflect the progress of the conversation.

In scenarios where workflow engines are used in an open environment, i.e., where workflows implementing different applications are offered as service to users, the characteristics of the actual workload executed by the engine are not known at the time the system is deployed. Thus, e.g., it may be difficult to choose between a centralized solution or a distributed implementation of the engine. Although a distributed engine may solve some of the scalability issues [9, 59], it opens up the problem of configuring the system in an optimal way. Considering the number of parameters involved and the variability of the workload, having a system administrator in charge of manually monitoring and reconfiguring the system does not seem a feasible solution.

To address this problem, we have in a first step designed and implemented a flexible platform for workflow execution as part of the JOpera project [88] which achieves scalability by replicating its key components across a cluster of computers. Additionally, the system incorporates autonomic computing principles [61] such as self-configuration, self-optimization and self-healing [49]. The system employs an autonomic controller in order to remove the need for manual configuration. This controller monitors the current workload and state of the system. It uses this information to determine whether the system is running in the optimal configuration or, alternatively, whether reconfiguration actions [87] have to be carried out. For example, if a peak of workflow execution requests is detected, more nodes of the cluster are allocated to process them.

To define the behavior of the autonomic controller, we have developed basic policies [93]. These policies can be chosen according to different goals (e.g., minimize resource allocation or minimize response time). While such policies define how the autonomic controller reacts to changes in the workload by adapting its configuration, its exact behavior depends on configurations using thresholds. Using such threshold-based policies is only a partial solution to the self-configuration problem: if it is difficult to set the optimal configuration of a system, optimally configuring an autonomic controller with such thresholds is an even harder problem [15].

As an example, in our experience with the JOpera autonomic workflow engine, we observed a 287% performance variation depending on the values of thresholds used by the autonomic controller policies, which is similar to the performance variation of a misconfigured engine.

Autonomic controllers that require to be configured – with parameters, thresholds, or 'if-then' rules – defeat the goal of automatic self-configuration and do not really help system administrators to deal with the complexity of managing their systems [62]. Instead, they potentially make it even more complex to manage a system, due to the need of understanding the impact of the controller configuration parameters on the overall system performance.

As a first step to work towards zero-configuration policies, we have looked at standardized controllers and implemented a PID policy [53], for which specific configuration and tuning techniques are available. If however the characteristics of the system or the workload change, the PID controller may need to be tuned again. Starting from an analytical model of the system under control, we therefore have also developed a zero-configuration policy removing any need for configuration [48].

The remainder of this part is structured as follows. The rest of this chapter discusses related work. In Chapter 7, the architecture of JOpera, the workflow engine we have used to implement the autonomic extensions, is presented. In the same chapter we also describe how JOpera can be replicated across a cluster and motivate with measurements our further work by showing how difficult it is to find a suitable configuration of the distributed execution engine for a given workload. We subsequently describe capabilities and architecture of the system with the autonomic controller (Chapter 8) and illustrate the feasibility of the approach. In the next chapter (Chapter 9) we then present the basic, threshold-based policies which can be used to define the behavior of the autonomic controller. We then gradually remove any need to configure the policies, working towards zero-configuration policies and discuss the resulting policies in Chapter 10. We conclude this part of the book with conclusions in Chapter 11.

6.2. Related Work

Decentralization of workflow process execution is an important area of research. Typically this is done to support business processes across companies without having to use a centralized entity [21]. This type of process decentralization can lead to higher throughput but it also introduces several problems on its own such as the lack of a global view over the process. It also does not address the scalability and reliability problems

6. Introduction

per se since the problem is simply translated to each node that executes parts of the process.

A large amount of research results is available in the context of scalable process execution engines (e.g.,[9, 21, 52, 59, 91]). However, given the design of a distributed engine, the practical problem of how to configure it at runtime in order to achieve good performance under different workload conditions is still poorly understood. As an example, the GOLIAT [40] tool uses the expected characteristics of the workload to make predictions about the performance of a certain configuration of the Mentor-lite engine. At deployment time, the tool helps the user to determine interactively how many resources should be allocated to achieve the desired level of performance.

In [60] an approach to self-optimizing computer systems has been developed. The approach uses an online control algorithm which relies on workload prediction to optimally reconfigure a Web server with respect to QoS goals over a limited time horizon. The problem of adaptively replicating functionality to achieve higher throughput has also been identified by the database community (e.g. [46, 121]): unbounded replication of functionality can lead to performance losses. The challenge therefore is to replicate distinct functionality depending on the workload only when required.

We on the other hand propose to use autonomic principles [58] to determine the configuration of the distributed engine automatically, taking into account measurements of the system's performance under the actual (and unpredictable) workload. Furthermore, with our approach it is not required to allocate resources to the engine on a permanent basis, as the autonomic controller can grow and shrink the system dynamically using whatever shared resources are available at the moment. In this context, the problem of optimally choosing which resource to use is dual to a resource management and scheduling problem (e.g., [101]): whereas a scheduler attempts to fit the workload to the available resources, the goal of the autonomic controller is to adapt the configuration of the resources to better service the workload.

Reducing or removing configuration and maintenance overhead, zero-configuration is a very important requirement for improving the acceptance and usability of systems. This has been recognized, for example, in the area of networking for some time [22].

In the context of autonomic computing, the problem and the difficulty of configuring controllers based on low-level performance indicators has been recognized [15]. The use of higher-level policies and goals has also been studied [62]. Other approaches [78] express the goals in the form of quality of service parameters which need to be set to define the behavior of the system. Using these parameters, a QoS controller estimates the QoS provided by the system in the short-term, matches it with the desired QoS and performs configuration changes to optimize the system with respect to the QoS goal. In our approach, we propose to employ policies that remove the need for any configuration of the controller.

A more holistic approach [65] goes beyond reconfiguring the engine and also targets at reconfiguring the complete environment: possible reconfiguration actions for instance also include moving services used by the workflow between nodes. Instead of reconfiguring the engine, also the workflow can be reconfigured in order to react to a changing

6. Introduction

environment [8]. Using late binding, the services used by the workflow are determined during execution through metadata attached to the workflow.

7. Background

In this chapter we motivate our work on autonomic computing applied to workflow execution engines. We will use the following definition of a workflows in the remainder of this part. Workflow processes (or workflows) model the interactions between different tasks by defining the data flow and control flow between them. The data flow defines data exchanges between tasks whereas the control flow constrains the order of task invocations [39].

With this, we first outline the architecture of JOpera, the workflow execution engine we have extended as part of the work presented in this book, in Section 7.1. We then discuss how the functionality of JOpera can be replicated on a cluster of computers to allow for scalable workflow execution in Section 7.1.2. With the distribution of the functionality however also comes the question of how to configure the distributed engine. Different workloads may require different configurations of the engine to execute a given workload fast as we illustrate in Section 7.2. From this we develop requirements for an autonomic controller which will adapt the engine's configuration to characteristics of the current workload (Section 7.2.3).

7.1. Workflow Execution Engine Architecture

The execution of a process begins with a request sent through the corresponding API of the engine. Processes can be started by users or can be invoked from other processes (as recursively called subprocesses). The engine API queues such requests into the *process execution requests* space (or process space). As shown in Figure 7.1, these requests are handled by the navigator, which 1) creates a new workflow instance into the *process execution state* space and 2) begins with the actual enactment of the workflow. To do so, the navigator uses the current state of the execution of a process to determine which tasks should be invoked next based on the control and data flow dependencies that are triggered by the completion of the previous tasks. Once the navigator determines that a certain task is ready to be invoked, the corresponding tuple is stored in the *task execution request space* (or task space).

The invocation of the tasks is managed by the *dispatcher* component. The name of this component is derived from its function of executing tasks by dispatching messages to and from the corresponding service providers. These include, e.g. worklist handlers for tasks that should be carried out by human operators, but also standard compliant Web services, as well as many other kinds of services [89]. After the execution of the task has been finished, the dispatcher notifies the navigator through the *event space*. More precisely, the dispatcher packages the results of the invocation into a task completion

7. Background

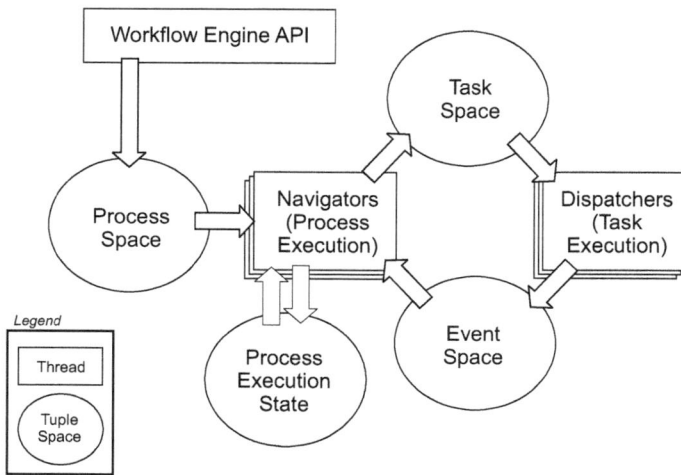

Figure 7.1.: Logical architecture of the JOpera distributed workflow execution engine

tuple, which is posted into the event space. Such tuples are then consumed by the navigator in order to update the state of the execution of the corresponding process and carry on with its execution.

The main reason for separating the execution of the workflows from the execution of their tasks lies in the observation that these operations have a different level of granularity. It is to be expected that the execution of task performed by the dispatcher may last significantly longer than the time taken by the navigator for scheduling it. With our approach, the platform supports the parallel invocation of multiple tasks belonging to the same process. Furthermore, a slow task does not affect the execution of other processes running concurrently because these two operations are handled asynchronously by different threads. This is already an important departure from existing workflow engines where navigation and dispatching are serially executed by a single thread.

7.1.1. Distributed Workflow Execution

Decoupling process navigation from task invocation enables the system to scale along two orthogonal directions. In case a large task invocation capacity is required, the dispatcher thread can be replicated across multiple nodes to manage the concurrent invocation of multiple tasks. Likewise, if many processes have to be executed concurrently, the navigator can also be replicated. The resulting pool of navigator and dispatcher threads are loosely coupled by using tuple spaces as depicted in Figure 7.1. We have chosen to use tuple spaces primarily for their persistent data storage capabilities as well as for the

7. Background

simple API provided. This way, navigators generate tuples containing task execution requests which are consumed by the dispatchers. Similarly, dispatchers send tuples back to the navigators to notify them of the results of the invocations. Thus, it is possible to scale the system to run on a cluster of computers, as navigators and dispatchers can be physically located on different nodes. However, at most one thread (dispatcher or navigator) is running on a node at a given time.

Tuple space also provide flexibility. First, thanks to their flexibility, it becomes feasible to dynamically reconfigure the system, as the number of navigators and dispatchers can be increased or decreased without having to stop the whole system. To do so, the system offers a reconfiguration API that makes it possible to control which thread is running on each node of the cluster. Second, tuple spaces also offer a convenient mechanism for instrumenting the system in order to gather performance information that can be fed back into the self-tuning algorithm of the autonomic controller. Third, they also provide flexibility with respect to their access semantics as one can configure the tuple space to return tuples with FIFO, LIFO or other queue semantics.

7.1.2. Scalable Workflow Execution

Although tuple spaces offer good abstractions for decoupling and replicating the navigator and dispatcher threads they pose a potential scalability bottleneck [85]. To address this problem, we use several layers of caching between the tuple space and the threads producing and consuming tuples. As this optimization affects the self-configuration mechanisms, in this section we describe it in more detail.

Instead of running only one tuple space server on a dedicated node, the distributed workflow engine replicates such tuple space server on each node of the cluster. One of the replicas is then configured to act as the global space, while all of the others are considered to be local with respect to the thread that is running on a particular node (Figure 7.2).

When a tuple is written by a thread, its destination is chosen in order to place it as closely as possible to the consumer. Thus, if a navigator posts an event to itself (e.g., when a workflow calls another workflow), the corresponding tuple is written in the local memory cache. However, if a dispatcher should notify a navigator of a completed task execution, the dispatcher will write a tuple in the space which is nearest to the receiving navigator, i.e., its local one. In all other cases the tuple is written in the global space. With the added complexity of maintaining a routing table which defines in which space the tuples should be written into, these optimizations help to reduce the load on the global tuple space [91].

This routing table is also used when reading tuples. In order to increase the throughput of the threads, each thread pre-fetches into its memory cache all relevant tuples, which are located both in the local and global spaces. This way, the tuples are immediately available when a thread is ready to take one.

The routing table contains a mapping between the ID of a process instance and the address of the node on which the navigator thread executing this process instance is located. This mapping is created when a navigator thread first begins running a particular

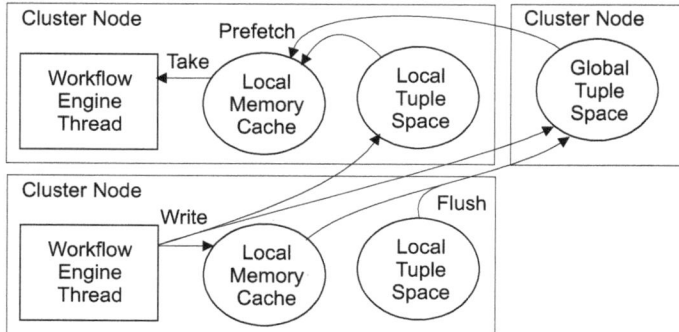

Figure 7.2.: Layers of caching between each thread and the global tuple space

process and is removed when the process is finished. However, if a system reconfiguration occurs and a navigator thread should be stopped, such mapping is also temporarily removed so that tuples are routed to the global space until the process execution is migrated to a different node. Also in this case, all cached tuples are flushed to the global space. The tuples flushed into the global space will be later picked up by a navigator continuing working on the according workflow execution.

7.2. Performance Evaluation

In this section we show that the optimal configuration of the distributed engine (in terms of the number of navigator and dispatcher threads that are used) is highly sensitive to its workload. Thus, it is important to be able to change the configuration of the engine in order to optimally service workloads with different characteristics.

For the following experiments, JOpera has been deployed on a cluster of up to 20 nodes. Each node is a 1.0GHz dual P-III, with 1 GB of RAM, running Linux (Kernel version 2.4.22) and Sun's Java Development Kit version 1.4.2. One additional node was allocated to run the global tuple space server, running IBM's T-Spaces v2.1.3 [57].

7. Background

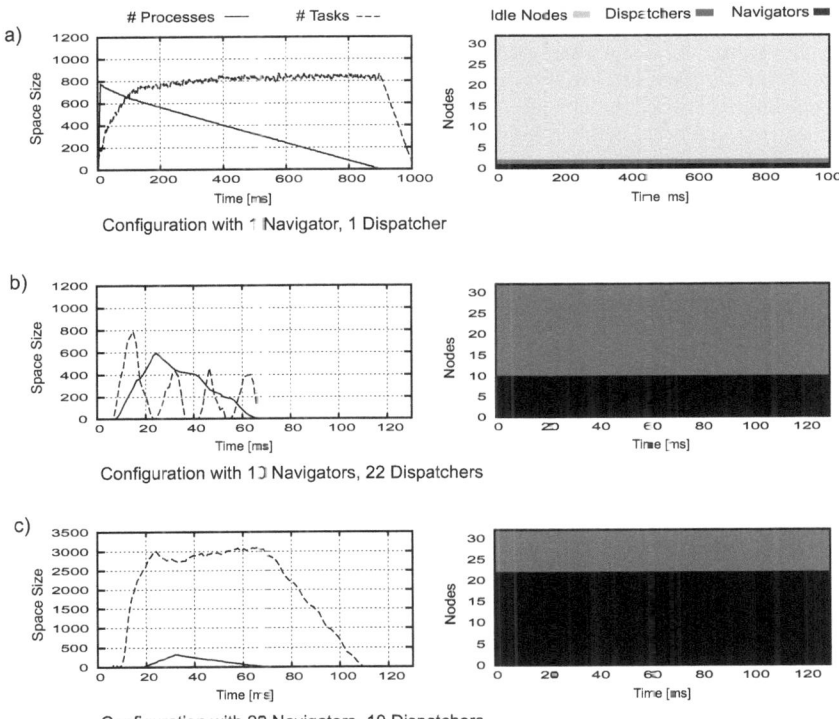

Figure 7.3.: Execution traces for a workload of 800 processes with three different configurations.

7.2.1. Scalability

The first set of results demonstrates the scalability of JCpera. An engine, configured to use only 1 dispatcher and 1 navigator, takes 973.22s to execute 800 concurrent processes of 10 parallel tasks, lasting 8 seconds (Figure 7.3a). For the same workload, this time drops to 73.13s when the engine is configured to use 10 navigator and 22 dispatcher threads.

This *static 22/10* configuration is suitable to run this kind of workload (Figure 7.3b). At the time the 800 processes are started, the system has already enough capacity to cope with them. Also, the system is balanced in terms of the number of each kind of thread so that it can handle the execution of both processes and tasks.

7. Background

However, misconfiguring the system may lead to a performance penalty. This can be seen in Figure 7.3c, where a *static 10/22* configuration of 22 navigator and 10 dispatcher threads has been used to execute the same workload. With this configuration, there is an imbalance between the number of navigators and dispatchers, as so few dispatchers cannot cope with the task tuples generated by so many navigators. As opposed to Figure 7.3b, where the task space oscillates up to 800 tuples, with this configuration, the task space reaches a peak of 3000 tuples. This imbalance is also reflected in the overall execution, which is delayed by 42.9 seconds or 60.2% compared to the *static 22/10* configuration.

These simple results already give an intuition of the difficulty of manually configuring the distributed engine. A mistake can lead to longer process execution times and suboptimal resource allocation.

7.2.2. Finding the Optimal Configuration

In order to find the configuration which minimizes the response time of the system for a given workload, we have carried out another series of experiments using different configurations. Figure 7.4 depicts the total execution times of two different workloads: 1000 concurrent processes containing 10 parallel tasks of the duration of 0 seconds (workload 0) and 1000 processes containing 10 parallel tasks of the duration of 20 seconds (workload 20). A total of 15 nodes were used in the experiments and all possible configurations starting with 14 navigators and 1 dispatcher up to 14 dispatchers and 1 navigator were tested.

The speedup profile shown on the right side of Figure 7.4 clearly illustrate that the optimal configuration for the two workloads is not the same. For workload 20, the optimal configuration is the one using 9 dispatchers and 6 navigators while for workload 0 the best configuration is the one using 5 dispatchers and 10 navigators. On the one hand, in the worst case the penalty of a misconfigured system is a factor of 5 in performance. On the other hand, if the system is optimally configured to handle one workload, its performance will suffer when it is subjected to a different one.

This can be illustrated with the following experiment. If we take both of the optimal configurations and use them to run a combined workload of two peaks separated by 120 seconds, the first consisting of workload 0 and the second of workload 20. With the configuration optimal for running workload 0, the time is 826 seconds, while the other configuration is faster with only 758 seconds.

Configuring the system statically therefore has two main problems. First, static configuration potentially leads to inefficient resource allocation, since the engine could release part of the cluster after processing a surge of requests. Second, a given configuration may not be optimal to deal with all kinds of workloads, hence reconfiguration is still required. In practice, such reconfiguration is quite difficult to perform manually. With the approach presented in the next chapter of this book, we show that it can be done automatically.

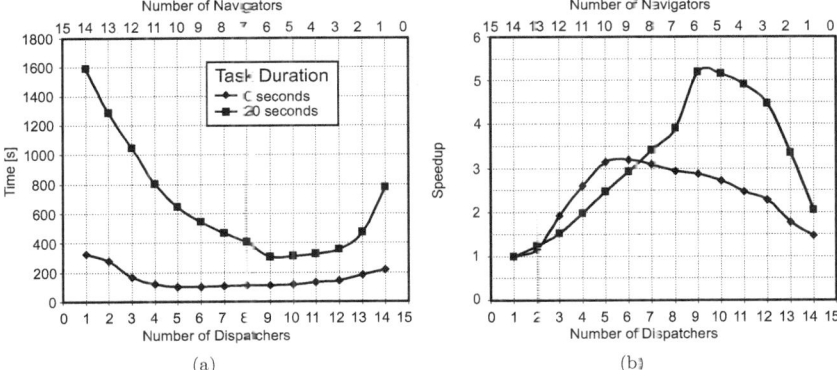

Figure 7.4.: Time required to execute two different workloads of 1000 processes using all possible static configurations (a) and speedup achieved relative to the slowest configuration (b)

7.2.3. Autonomic Requirements

As has been shown with experiments before, different workloads require different configurations. If such a workflow execution engine is run in an open environment it needs to be reconfigured on the fly in order to adapt to changing workloads. We therefore want to employ autonomic computing principles to allow the workflow execution engine to react to external events. To support autonomic behavior, the workflow execution engine must feature self-configuration and self-tuning to deal with changes in the workload as well as self-healing capabilities to deal with external events such as node failures.

Self-configuration entails switching the system's configuration on the fly without manual intervention and, most importantly, without disrupting the system. This requires the workflow execution engine to provide mechanisms to expose the state of its configuration as well as to support means to dynamically and efficiently change the configuration.

The **self-tuning** capabilities should ensure that system reconfiguration leads to a configuration which is optimal given the current workload. In order to enable self-tuning capabilities the workflow engine must give access to its internal state such that control algorithms can analyze current and past performance information in order to plan configuration changes in response to the current workload. Our assumption is that the characteristics of the workload affect the system's performance and that the self-tuning algorithm can optimally adapt the system to the workload by monitoring key performance indicators.

Finally, the system also needs to provide **self-healing** capabilities [100]. This means that it should be able to detect configuration changes due to external events, such as failures of nodes. If a discrepancy between the model of the configuration and the actual configuration is detected, the self-healing functionality should perform the necessary recovery actions. From this, we identify the requirement to support mechanisms for detecting failures and configuration changes of the cluster and to query the workflow execution state in order to determine how the running processes have been affected.

8. Autonomic Controller

In this chapter we will present the autonomic controller in charge of reconfiguring the system on the fly, reacting to changes in the workload and the distributed engine. We will first introduce the architecture of the autonomic controller in Section 8.1, describing in detail the self-tuning, self configuration and self-healing components and how they interact. We will then continue (Section 8.2) and show with a first set of basic experiments that the system will indeed be configured on the fly adapting itself to the current workload characteristics. As these experiments also show, having the distributed engine reconfigure the system on the fly improves the performance compared with a manually and statically configure engine.

8.1. Autonomic Capabilities

In this section we describe the design of the autonomic controller of the workflow engine. Figure 8.1 gives an overview over its main components (self-tuning, self-configuration, and self-healing) and the interactions between them.

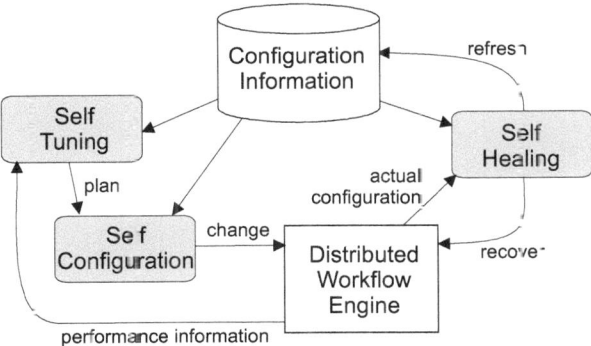

Figure 8.1.: Interaction between the components of the autonomic controller

The self-tuning and the self-configuration components interact closely, as the latter implements the configuration plan proposed by the former. The control loop connecting these two components is shown in Figure 8.2. First the self-tuning measures the system's performance and based on the new information, it decides whether a reconfiguration is

8. Autonomic Controller

needed. The configuration changes are implemented by the self-configuration component by choosing which nodes of the cluster will be affected. It is worth noting that it may not always be possible to apply all reconfiguration decisions, as these are constrained by the amount of available resources. After a change has been applied, its effects may not be immediately visible. Hence, to avoid repeating the same decisions based on out of date information, the controller waits for changes to take effect before restarting the loop.

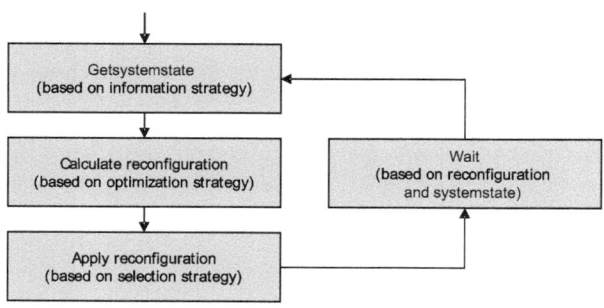

Figure 8.2.: Steps taken by the controller

The self-healing component on the other hand operates rather autonomously. It checks periodically for discrepancies in the configuration information and the actual configuration of the distributed engine. Differences are assumed to be failures and this component will restart failed dispatchers and navigators and resume the work executed on them.

8.1.1. Self-Tuning

The self-tuning component is responsible for determining whether the current system configuration is optimal. In case an imbalance is detected and a change of configuration is needed, the self-tuning component submits a reconfiguration plan to the self-configuration component. To do so, the self-tuning component acts upon three different strategies. The information strategy describes which performance indicators should be monitored in order to enhance the overall performance of the system. The optimization strategy defines how to achieve an optimal configuration, i.e., an optimal partitioning of the cluster between navigator and dispatcher threads. The selection strategy describes how to map the reconfiguration decision onto the cluster.

Information Strategy

By considering the architecture of the workflow engine (Figure 7.1), there are several points that can be instrumented to provide performance indicators. For example, since

8. Autonomic Controller

the navigator and dispatcher threads communicate asynchronously through tuple spaces, it is possible to sample the current *space size* in order to detect whether the system is balanced. In case the size of the space grows, it is likely that there are not enough consumers processing its tuples and too many producers of tuples. Conversely, if the size of a space decreases, there may be too many consumers (or too few producers). The information strategy therefore defines that the variation in the size of the tuple spaces of tasks and processes should be monitored to detect imbalances in the system's configuration.

Optimization Strategy

The goal of the optimization strategy is to establish a configuration such that the number of navigator and dispatcher threads is balanced. Since navigator threads produce task invocation requests and dispatcher threads consume them, the task tuple space is solely influenced by the internal system's configuration defined in terms of the number of dispatchers and navigators. This does not hold for the process tuple space where processes are submitted by the API and which is therefore subject to external influences which are independent of the configuration of the system.

The optimization strategy thus defines that the number of dispatcher threads needs to be increased when the rate of growth of the task space exceeds a certain threshold. Similarly, if the size of the process space increases, additional navigator threads should be started in order to execute the newly started processes. Given the limited number of available resources, the optimization strategy must determine how many nodes should be allocated to run navigators and how many should run dispatchers threads. Therefore, in case there are no idle nodes left, a navigator (or dispatcher) thread needs to be stopped in order to free a node for starting a dispatcher (or navigator). Stopping a navigator implies less task production capacity and starting a dispatcher means more task consumption capacity. Thus, switching from a navigator to a dispatcher thread effectively reduces the growth of the task space. Conversely, if all navigators are busy handling task completion notifications, the size of the process space will grow and additional navigators are required to execute the newly started processes.

Selection Strategy

Once the optimization strategy has determined the new configuration of the system, the selection strategy compares the new configuration with the current one in order to establish what nodes and threads should be affected by the planned configuration change.

Arriving at a concrete configuration that is to be submitted to the self-configuration component from an abstract configuration plan is done by prioritizing nodes according to how well suited they are for a configuration change. If there are idle nodes available and threads need to be started, the idle ones get the highest priority and are selected for the configuration change. Similarly, if there are more threads than necessary, idle threads should be the ones stopped. However, if all threads are busy and there are no

8. Autonomic Controller

more idle nodes, some need to be selected in order to apply the configuration change. For example, if an additional navigator thread needs to be started, a dispatcher thread will have to be stopped and vice versa.

Stopping non-idle threads may be expensive and the selection strategy therefore needs to take this reconfiguration cost into account when deciding which thread should be stopped. The *simple* selection strategy chooses the threads randomly, regardless of the resulting rescheduling overhead. However, we also experimented with a *smart* selection strategy that chooses threads with the goal of minimizing the overhead caused by rescheduled tasks and processes. In this case, threads are further prioritized by the number of tasks (or processes) that they are currently executing. With this heuristic, threads which are running many processes (or many tasks) are less likely to be interrupted, thus less work will have to be migrated to a different node.

8.1.2. Self-Configuration

As outlined in the previous section, the self-tuning component suggests a new, optimal configuration for the cluster. It is up to the self-configuration component to execute the actual reconfiguration of the cluster. For this purpose the self-configuration component captures the current configuration of the cluster and applies changes to it. Implementing the new configuration requires time and the result may not be available immediately.

In order to execute the reconfiguration plan, the self-configuration component uses a closed feedback-loop controller that takes as input the suggested configuration of the self-tuning component as well as the current configuration, as it is reported by the self-healing component. As threads are being stopped (or started) on remote nodes, this component periodically checks the progress of these reconfiguration actions and ensures that the new configuration is reached. If, in the meantime, the self-tuning component has suggested another reconfiguration plan, the execution of the current one will be interrupted.

Reconfiguration Actions

The self-configuration component can alter the configuration of the engine as follows:

Starting Threads:
In order to start a thread on a particular node, the JOpera API first needs to be started. The API waits for start and stop commands sent to it. Starting dispatcher and navigator threads can be done as long as the node is idle. The self-configuration component only needs to issue the start command on the node and the according thread will start working immediately.

Stopping Navigator Threads:
Stopping a navigator thread entails migrating the state of the processes the navigator thread is working on and redirecting associated events. Migrating the state of a process is done by flushing the locally cached state into the global tuple space so that a next

navigator can pick it up and resume working on it. All cached events which the navigator has not yet processed will also be transferred into the global tuple space. Furthermore, events that may be triggered by dispatcher threads executing task invocations that belong to a process that is about to be migrated, are redirected to the global event tuple space.

Stopping Dispatcher Threads:
In contrast to stopping navigators, stopping a dispatcher thread is more difficult. Dispatcher threads are executing tasks that may involve the invocation of a local application or the interaction with a remote service provider on the Web. In some cases, it may not be possible to transparently interrupt such executions. Processes can contain metadata that defines whether a task is repeatable, which can be used under these circumstances to choose the appropriate method.

More concretely, we take this into account by providing different methods of stopping a dispatcher thread. The *kill method* immediately stops all active task executions in progress on a particular dispatcher thread and ensures that all task invocations will be repeated on a different dispatcher thread by placing the corresponding tuple back in the task space. Repeating all tasks which have been executing introduces some overhead as the process execution is delayed. Clearly, this method can only be applied to repeatable or resumable tasks which are more likely to be found in scientific computing applications.

The *stop method* immediately ceases to take tuples from the task space. As a consequence, no new tasks will be started, but the dispatcher will wait for all task executions to finish before stopping. This method has the disadvantage that – as long as all tasks have not finished their execution – the node is not immediately available for starting a different thread. A dispatcher thread executing a mixture tasks. some requiring stop semantics while others require kill semantics, may only be interrupted using the stop method. The engine therefore schedules tasks with kill semantics on specific dispatcher threads which can then be stopped immediately allowing faster reconfiguration of the system.

8.1.3. Self-Healing

Independent of the other two components, the task of the self-healing component is to ensure that the workflow engine remains in a consistent state in spite of external events affecting its configuration. To do so, the component periodically monitors the nodes of the cluster, checks their availability and compares their state with the information stored in the configuration space. In addition to this pull strategy, we also keep the configuration information up-to-date by having the newly started threads register with the configuration state autonomously. A failure is thus detected as a mismatch between the known configuration and the actual configuration of the cluster. If a failure occurs, the component ensures that the affected processes and tasks are correctly recovered by the rest of the workflow engine. More precisely, failures are handled differently, depending on what kind of thread has failed.

Handling Dispatcher Thread Failures:
In case a dispatcher fails, the tasks that were managed by it are lost and have to be restarted. The self-healing component queries the state of the execution of the process to determine which were the tasks currently assigned to the failed thread. These tasks are automatically restarted by resubmitting the corresponding task into the task execution request space. This recovery procedure is very similar to the one carried out when the self-configuration component kills a dispatcher in order to reconfigure the system. Also in that case, some tasks may have to be re-executed.

Handling Navigator Thread Failures: Should a navigator thread fail, the state of the execution of the process is still available in the global process execution state space because the navigators perform work only on a cached copy of the state. The self-healing component can recover the processes by simply removing their entries in the tuple routing table which point to the failed navigator. This way, all pending events can be routed through the global space until another navigator becomes available to process them.

8.2. Autonomic Workflow Execution

The goal of this first system evaluation is to analyze the autonomic capabilities of the workflow engine. In particular, we want to explore if and how the system is able to adapt to different workload conditions automatically and how it reacts to failures. In this first part we study how, given a workload as described in Section 7.2.2 (1000 concurrent processes containing 10 parallel tasks with a duration of 0 seconds (for workload 0) and with a duration of 20 seconds (for workload 20)), the autonomic controller reconfigures the system optimally by using the self-configuration as well as the self-tuning component.

Then we present an interesting self-healing result where the engine not only recovers the execution of its tasks, but can also re-balance its configuration to optimally use the nodes which remain available after a failure.

As a baseline to compare the results quantitatively, we have used the configurations optimal for workload 0 and workload 20 and have executed a combined workload of two peaks separated by 120 seconds, the first consisting of workload 0 and the second of workload 20. With the configuration optimal for running workload 0, the time is 826 seconds, while the other configuration is faster with only 758 seconds (Figure 8.3, right two columns). Figure 8.4 (left) shows the behavior of the system as it automatically adapts its configuration to different workloads. We first describe the trace of one experiment, obtained by sampling various performance indicators and logging their values at regular intervals (every second). Then, we compare different selection strategies combined with a different choice of reconfiguration actions to determine the corresponding reconfiguration overhead.

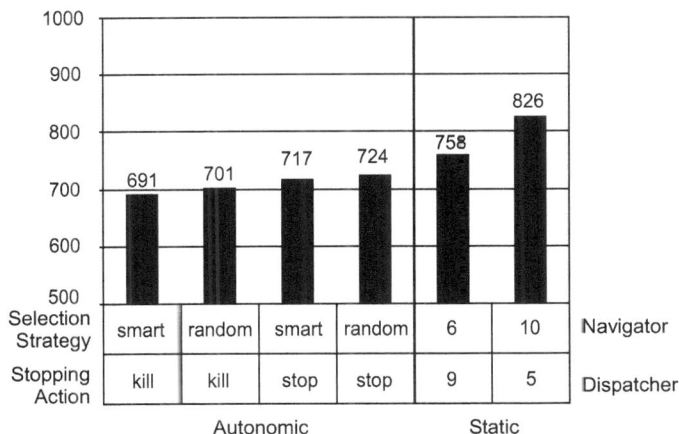

Figure 8.3.: Comparison of the execution time when using different strategies to run the combined workloads

8. Autonomic Controller

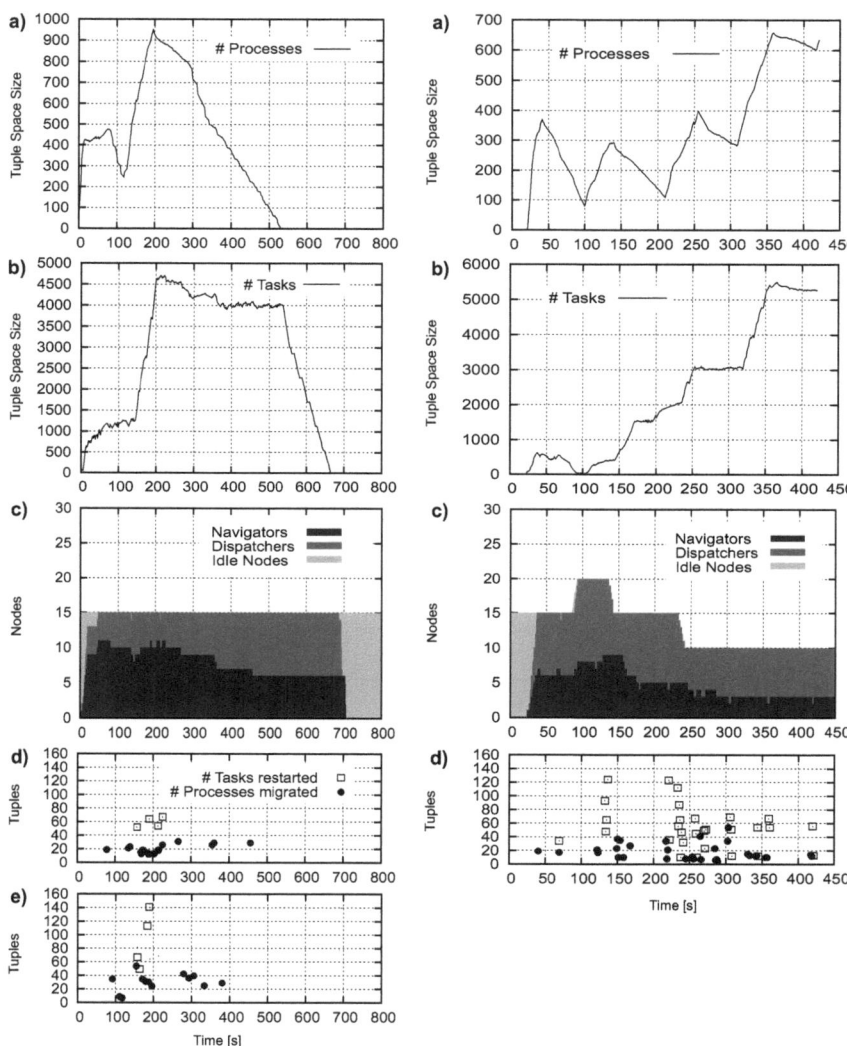

Figure 8.4.: Autonomic Controller reconfiguring the system as workload changes (left) & healing the system as nodes are added and removed (right)

8. *Autonomic Controller*

8.2.1. Self-Configuration

Figure 8.4a (left) shows the size of the *process execution requests* tuple space over time. This gives a good overview of the rate at which processes are queued to be started (the curve grows) and instantiated and executed by navigators (the curve drops). It also directly reflects the workload which is applied to the system, which – in this experiment – consists of two peaks with varying characteristics.

The first peak occurring at t=0 consists of 1000 processes which execute 10 parallel tasks having a duration of 0 seconds. The characteristic of the processes requires more navigators than dispatchers to be started: since the tasks can be executed in virtually no time, the dispatchers can execute many tasks in a given period of time. As the dispatchers can handle a lot of tasks, there is a need for a significant number of navigators handling their completion notifications as well as issuing new ones.

As can be seen in Figure 8.4(left) c, the controller configures the system accordingly by allocating only up to 5 dispatchers, while using the rest of the nodes to run navigators. This configuration will change as the second peak hits the system at t=120s when the number of processes that still wait to be executed is already declining. As can be seen in Figure 8.4(left) a, in response to this peak, the number of process execution requests waiting in the tuple space grows as the new processes are fed into the system.

As these processes begin their execution, the size of the task tuple space also starts to increase as a result (Figure 8.4(left) b). This can be explained by the different characteristics of the second peak. Although it still comprises of 1000 processes, executing 10 parallel tasks, the task duration has now been set to 20 seconds. Thus, more dispatchers are required, as tasks now take longer to run. Between t=150 and t=200, the controller attempts to balance a system which lags behind both in the execution of processes (at t=200, the number of waiting processes peaks at almost 1000) and in the execution of tasks. Thus, the configuration does not change significantly. Once all processes have been queued, Figure 8.4(left) c shows that actual reconfiguration starts after t=200. More precisely, the self-tuning algorithm detects the imbalance and begins to steadily increase the number of nodes allocated to the dispatcher threads, while reducing the number of navigator threads. The configuration eventually stabilizes after t=400s. The system is balanced again, as Figure 8.4(left) b shows: the number of tasks remains stable (4000) indicating that the number of consumers (the dispatchers) is balanced with the number of producers (the navigators).

At t=521, all processes have been started and thereby all the contained tasks have been put into the task execution request space. The number of tasks in the space steadily decreases thereafter. At second 691 all tasks have been executed and the controller stops the dispatchers as they become idle. Shortly afterward, the number of navigators reaches zero, because the self-configuration component also stops these threads as they become idle.

8. Autonomic Controller

Reconfiguration Overhead

Figure 8.4(left) d shows the reconfiguration overhead. Whenever a navigator is stopped, the cached state of its processes is transferred into a global tuple space waiting for a next navigator to pick it up. More significant is the overhead introduced by stopping dispatchers. If a dispatcher is stopped, all tasks it has been executing are stopped and need to be repeated leading to a delay in the overall execution of their process.

In this experiment, we compare different selection strategies for choosing which thread running on what node should be stopped. The goal is to determine which strategy minimizes the reconfiguration overhead. First of all, we logged the number of tasks and processes that were rescheduled and migrated as the corresponding thread was stopped. From this, it can be seen that the *random* selection strategy (Figure 8.4(left) e) appears to reschedule more tasks and migrate more processes than the *smart* selection strategy (Figure 8.4(left) d). When running the same workload, the number of reconfiguration actions is approximately the same, but the height of the peaks is much lower, as the smart selection strategy chooses the nodes with the least amount of work to be repeated. This leads to an decrease of the overall execution time of 10.6 seconds (Figure 8.3).

In this figure we also combine the selection strategies with a different choice of reconfiguration actions (*kill* vs. *stop*). As the results indicate, the dominant factor regarding execution time is the reconfiguration action. Both selection strategies perform better by using the kill method instead of the stop method for stopping dispatcher threads. The reason for this is that when using the stop method, reconfiguration does not happen immediately. Instead, the dispatcher must wait until the longest task has been executed. In case of our experiments with tasks lasting up to 20 seconds, in the worst case reconfiguration was delayed by 20 seconds.

8.2.2. Self-Healing

The goal of the self-healing experiment is to demonstrate the ability of the system to react to external changes affecting the configuration of the cluster. In this experiment the system is initially configured to use 15 nodes. Then, in order to replace 5 of the nodes assigned to it, 5 additional nodes are added and a bit later a different group of 5 nodes is removed. Towards the end of the experiment, the newly added nodes fail.

This time the workload consists of four peaks of 500 processes occurring every 100 seconds. Each of the processes consist of 10 parallel tasks of 10 seconds duration. Starting with 15 nodes, the cluster has been grown to 20 nodes at t=90 and has then been reduced by 5 nodes at t=140 and again by 5 nodes at t=230. When the cluster grows by 5 nodes at t=90, the system instantly uses the additionally available nodes by increasing both the number of dispatcher as well as the number of navigator threads. The increase of the number of dispatchers leads to a the task space being empty temporarily at t=100 as can be seen in Figure 8.4(right) b. The task space is filled again soon because the process space starts to grow when the second peak of the workload is fed into the system.

At t=140 5 nodes running dispatchers are removed from the cluster. Because there is still the same number of navigators producing tasks but a smaller number of dispatchers

8. Autonomic Controller

consuming them, the task space starts to accumulate tuples at t=150 due to this imbalance. The system subsequently adapts to this situation by stopping navigators and starting dispatchers again between t=155 and t=170 as can be seen in Figure 8.4(right) c. The growth of the task space slows down shortly after the system has readjusted the configuration.

Figure 8.4(right) d illustrates the recovery actions performed by the self-healing component: at t=140 five dispatchers are stopped and therefore the tasks that were currently running are automatically rescheduled. Navigators were stopped when the system adapts to the new conditions and their processes were rescheduled shortly after t=150.

The third configuration change at t=230 also involves the loss of 5 dispatchers. The system reacts consistently. Reducing the dispatchers while leaving the number of navigators leads to a growth of the task space which in turn triggers a reconfiguration. The system will subsequently reduce the number of navigators and increase the number of dispatchers. This change in configuration will again contain the growth of the task space. The change of the configuration can again be observed in Figure 8.4(right) d where after the degradation by 5 dispatchers tasks are rescheduled at t=230. At t=250 processes are rescheduled due to the configuration change which entails stopping navigators and starting dispatchers.

The different configurations are also reflected in Figure 8.4(right) d: because the number of navigators changes, the slope of the process space also changes. When for instance comparing the number of navigators between t=40–100, t=130–210 and t=260–320, one can observe that the slope of the process space size curve becomes flatter. This is a result of the number of navigators gradually being smaller.

Since there are no additional workload peaks occurring after second 310 the system will simply execute all processes and tasks until both spaces are empty with a stable configuration of 3 navigators and 7 dispatchers after t=450.

8.3. Conclusions

Although it is not impossible to find an optimal static configuration for a given workload, it is very difficult to assess the workload a priori and configure the system accordingly. In our first experiments we have been able to tune the configurations in order to execute a given workload as optimally as possible. But workloads with different characteristics lead to different optimal configurations as had been shown in the previous chapter in Figure 7.4. And if a statically configured system executes a workload with characteristics it has not been tuned for, its performance degrades. To overcome this, either manual reconfiguration or self-tuning plus self-configuration is required.

As the results of the self-configuration experiment indicate, the autonomic controller was able to adapt the configuration of the workflow engine according to the variable characteristics of the workload. By combining the workloads of the base line experiments, the autonomic controller shifted the system's configuration between the optimal static ones. This had an impact on the overall performance, as the comparison between differ-

8. Autonomic Controller

ent versions of the autonomic controller and the optimal static configurations indicated (Figure 8.3).

As expected, the smart selection strategy outperformed the random selection strategy. With it, the impact of a reconfiguration is minimized, as the least number of tasks have to be restarted when stopping a dispatcher. Combining the smart selection strategy for stopping threads with the kill reconfiguration action leads to the most significant speedup compared to the static configurations. Overall, for all combinations of a selection strategy with a stopping action the autonomic engine performed better than a statically configured one.

The self-healing experiment reflects a common situation in the lifetime of a cluster-based system, where nodes are rotated as some of them may have to be taken off-line for maintenance. With traditional systems, such intervention would require to manually determine which parts of the engine would be affected by the reconfiguration and manually stop the components running on the nodes to be replaced. As we have shown in the previous section, the autonomic controller was able to immediately detect the newly assigned nodes and could also transparently recover and optimally reconfigure the engine when some of the nodes were taken off-line.

In the followings chapter we will use the autonomic controller as a basis and develop policies to define its behavior. With different such policies, the autonomic controller can be configured to work towards different goals. We will first present a set of basic policies which themselves still require some configuration and will then develop policies which do not require any configuration at all.

9. Basic Policies

The behavior of the autonomic controller can be defined by using different policies which can be chosen according to different goals (e.g., minimize resource allocation or minimize response time). Such a policy is, as discussed in Section 8.1, defined by a selection strategy, information strategy and at its core, an optimization strategy. In this chapter we will first define and evaluate a first set of basic policies which have common information and selection strategies, but differ with respect to the optimization strategy working towards different goals. In Section 9.1 we therefore first describe the common information and selection strategies and discuss different optimization strategies. We will then move on to evaluate these optimization strategies in Section 9.2 and conclude in Section 9.3.

9.1. Threshold-Based Policies

9.1.1. Information Strategy

The information strategy defines which performance indicators and which part of the configuration information are fed back into the autonomic controller.

For the threshold-based policies presented in this chapter we use the size of both spaces as an indicator. If there is a variation in the space size, i.e., it grows or shrinks, then the system is not balanced and may require reconfiguration. If the task space grows, then there are either too many navigators or too little dispatchers. If the task space shrinks, then there are either too many dispatchers or too little navigators. The case of the event space is analogous.

In order to compare the performance of different optimization strategies, it is also useful to measure their corresponding *resource allocation*. To do so, the system tracks for how long it has been using a certain node of the cluster. These allocation logs are kept as part of the configuration information.

9.1.2. Optimization Strategy

The optimization strategy specifies how to achieve certain goals in terms of mapping a combination of the previously defined performance indicators onto the previously discussed reconfiguration actions.

In general, the controller addresses multiple (and contradictory) goals. First of all, it should ensure that the system reacts with reasonable performance under a given workload. The simplest way to achieve this points to a strategy that configures the system to always provide excess capacity so that unpredictable peaks in the workload can be absorbed. Although this approach maximizes the performance of the system measured in term of its process execution capacity, it turns out to be wasteful in terms of resource allocation. Thus, the optimization strategy must provide support for both of these goals: maximizing the system's throughput and minimizing the resource allocation. The simplest optimization strategy we have considered uses a single threshold T compared to a certain non-negative controlled variable v. Whenever $v > T$ the controller decides to grow the size of the system by one thread. This ensures that peaks in the workload causing the controlled variable to increase will be detected and taken care of by growing the system. If $v = 0$, the outcome is to shrink the size of the system by one thread. No reconfiguration action is planned if $0 < v \leq T$.

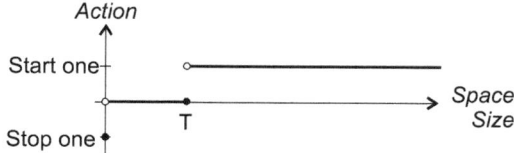

Figure 9.1.: *Simple* optimization strategy

We have applied this *simple* optimization strategy (Figure 9.1) by binding the controlled variable v to the size s of the space of events consumed by the navigators and the dispatchers and by introducing different thresholds (T_d, T_n) for each kind of thread. To tune their values, the thresholds can be interpreted as the number of events which is expected to be handled by each kind of thread. Typically $T_n > T_d$, as navigators can handle a larger volume of events than dispatchers.

As opposed to reading the current size of the event space, the *differential* optimization strategy (Figure 9.2) uses the first order variation ($\Delta s = s(t) - s(t-1)$) of the space size to make its decisions.

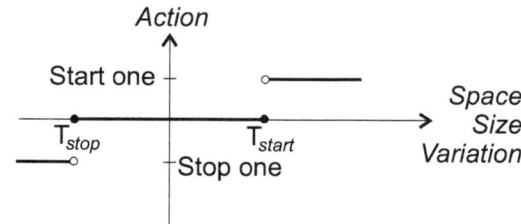

Figure 9.2.: *Differential* optimization strategy

9. Basic Policies

Still, the possible outcomes and the decision strategy are the same as in the simple optimization strategy. We introduced this strategy because the size of the event space is a good indicator of the internal activity of the system. Its variations can be used to detect whether the system is lagging behind (when $\Delta s > 0$) or the number of events to be processed is diminishing ($\Delta s < 0$). Thus, two different thresholds are used to determine whether a new thread should be started ($\Delta s > T_{start} > 0$) or stopped ($\Delta s < T_{stop} < 0$).

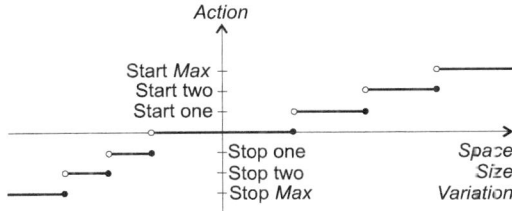

Figure 9.3.: *Proportional* optimization strategy

The *proportional* optimization strategy (Figure 9.3) uses a set of thresholds to determine whether one or more threads should be started or stopped, proportionally to Δs. To avoid instability problems, we set a limit to the maximum number of threads that can be started or stopped at once. This strategy also uses the previously described Δs as controlled variable, since it provides both positive and negative values that can be used as input into the control decisions. Compared to the simple and differential strategies, we expect this strategy to be more reactive, as it can plan to start many threads at once if a large variation in the workload is detected.

9.1.3. Selection Strategy

The selection strategy defines how to map abstract reconfiguration decisions to concrete actions affecting the current system configuration.

For the threshold based policies presented in this chapter we have used the following selection strategy. For growing the system, idle nodes are selected randomly, i.e. we use the simple selection strategy. For shrinking the system or reconfiguring a node we use the smart selection strategy, thereby selecting the thread stopping which introduces the least reconfiguration overhead as was discussed in Section 8.1.

9.2. Evaluation

The goal of the measurements is to evaluate the different optimization strategies, whereby the configuration of the system is adapted automatically to different workload conditions. We begin with a brief description of the characteristics of the workload.

9.2.1. Workload and Testbed Description

Since there are no standardized benchmarks for workflow execution platforms, we have defined a simple workload to evaluate the system under extreme conditions. The workload imposed on the system can be described as a peak of concurrent client requests to start the execution of a certain number of new processes. Thus, the *size* of the workload can be characterized by the number of processes to be executed concurrently. Although the number of tasks and the structure of the processes also influence the performance of the system, for these experiments we have focused on a homogeneous workload consisting of processes composed by 10 parallel tasks whose invocation time has been set to 8 seconds. We limited our experiments to this kind of workload because this simplifies the analysis of the results of our experiments and due to space limitations. We plan to continue the evaluation of the system with heterogeneous and continuous workloads as part of future work. For the experiments, JOpera has been deployed on a cluster of up to 32 nodes. Each node is a 1.0GHz dual P-III, with 1 GB of RAM, running Linux (Kernel version 2.4.22) and Sun's Java Development Kit version 1.4.2.

9.2.2. Static Configuration

For the following experiments we use a static configuration of 22 dispatchers and 10 navigators as a baseline to compare the other strategies to. This *static 22/10* configuration is suitable for this kind of workload: at the time when the processes are started, the system is able to cope with it. Enough threads are ready to handle the execution of both processes and tasks. An execution trace of this configuration is shown in Figure 9.5.

However, configuring the system statically reveals two main problems. First, static configuration potentially leads to a waste of resources since the cluster remains fully allocated to workflow execution engine although it would be possible to reduce the resource allocation after processing the surge. Second, as we have shown previously, the configuration may not be optimal to deal with all kinds of workloads, hence reconfiguration is still required. Manual reconfiguration is not a trivial task because misconfiguring the system may lead to a loss in performance, as can be seen when comparing the batch execution time achieved with the *static 22/10* and the *static 10/22* configurations for the same workload (Figure 9.4).

9.2.3. Autonomic Configuration

In order to compare the autonomic controller with a statically configured system, we have implemented and evaluated the strategies described in Section 9.1 using different workload sizes and configuring the control algorithm to run every second.

Simple Optimization Strategy:
The *simple* optimization strategy configures the system by adding one navigator thread at a time to the configuration as long as the size of the process space exceeds the thresh-

9. Basic Policies

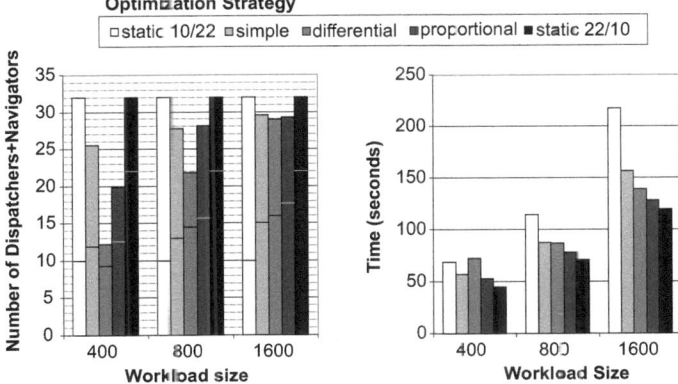

Figure 9.4.: Comparison of the strategies regarding resource utilization (left) and process execution time (right)

old $T_n = 50$. The same holds with $T_d = 10$ for the dispatcher threads servicing the task space. Figure 9.5b shows the *simple* optimization strategy responding to a peak of 800 processes. Although the process space is filled up quickly, the configuration adapts only slowly. The size of the task space grows comparatively big because of the large number of navigator threads that are active as soon as the configuration has grown to its maximum size. The *simple* optimization strategy attempts to grow the configuration as long as the space sizes are bigger than T_n and T_d. Given the values of the thresholds, this happens during most of the experiment's duration.

Differential Optimization Strategy:

Instead of only considering the size of the space, the *differential* optimization strategy takes the growth of the space into consideration. Once the growth of the task space has overstepped the T^d_{start} threshold (set to 10 in this experiment), one dispatcher thread is added to the configuration. Vice versa, if the variation of the space size is below $T^d_{stop} = -10$, a dispatcher is removed from the configuration. The same mechanism applies to navigator threads, except that $T^n_{start} = 50$, $T^n_{stop} = -50$. As it can be seen in Figure 9.5c, this optimization strategy adapts to the current workload without letting the system constantly grow until saturation is reached. Instead, the growth of the system is coupled with the growth of the workload. The thresholds chosen allows the controller to follow small variations in the workload. Small increases of the task space size result in an increase in the number of dispatcher threads.

Proportional Optimization Strategy:

9. Basic Policies

The *proportional* optimization strategy tries to improve the reaction time of the system. In contrast to the *simple* and *differential* optimization strategy, the *proportional* optimization strategy adds or removes a variable (but limited) number of threads to the current configuration proportionally to the variation of the space. The magnitude of the reconfiguration actions has been limited to 3 navigators and 10 dispatchers. By adjusting the number of threads in larger increments, the system is able to adapt faster to the workload peak (Figure 9.5d). Given the initial surge of the process space, the system reaches a stable configuration much faster by quickly increasing the number of navigators and in turn also the number of dispatchers. Similar to the *simple* optimization strategy, the size of the task space remains quite high in this case as well, as the configuration uses a large number of navigators. However, the controller reacts to this by adding more dispatchers, causing a drop in the task space (Figure 9.5d, seconds 6, 12 and 24).

9. Basic Policies

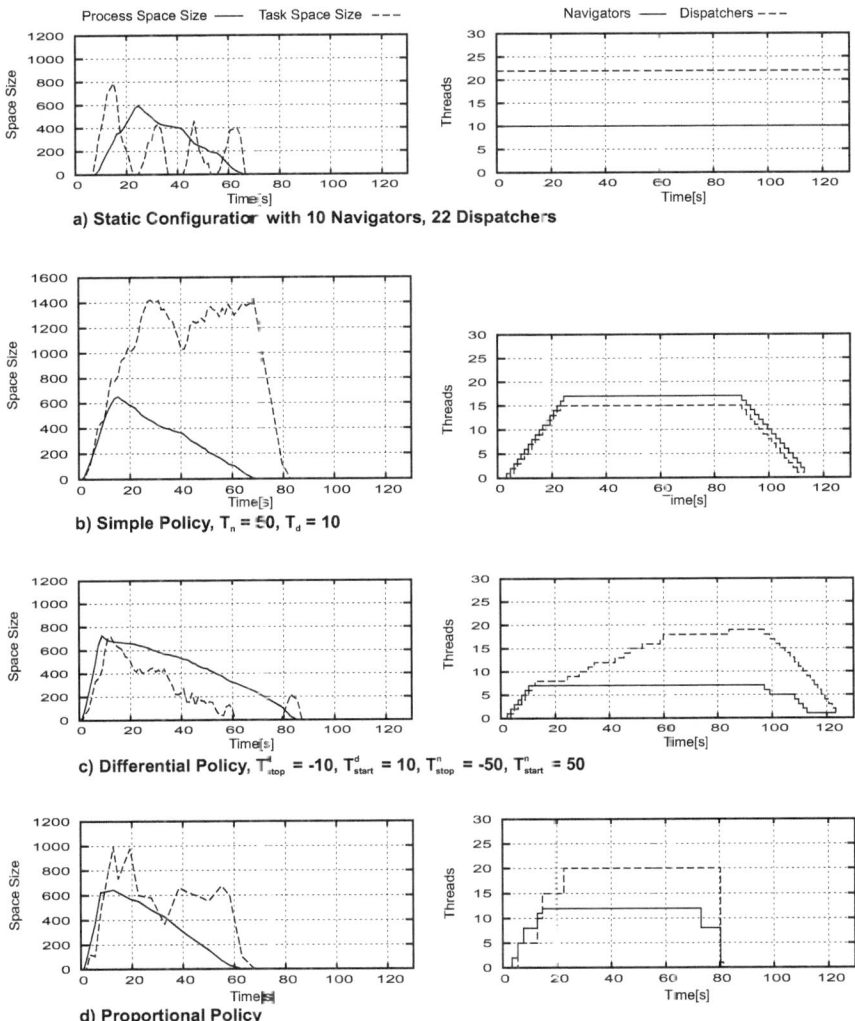

Figure 9.5.: Traces of the size of the spaces (left) and the state of the configuration (right) with different optimization strategies reacting to a workload peak of 800 concurrent processes

9. Basic Policies

9.2.4. Comparison of the Optimization Strategies

In order to develop an idea about how well the different strategies perform, we have evaluated the strategies regarding the time used to execute batches of 400, 800 and 1600 processes and the average resource allocation over this time. Figure 9.4 gives an overview of the results.

The time for executing a batch was measured as the time between the time when the first process execution request is put in the process space and the time the execution of the last process was completed. The average resource allocation was measured as the sum of the time each of the nodes was running a JOpera thread divided by the duration of the batch.

Not surprisingly, the average resource allocation for the two static configurations, with 22 dispatchers and 10 navigators and vice versa, is 32. A more interesting result is that, although the same number of nodes is used, the time to execute the same batch is between 50% (batch size 400 processes) and 82% (batch size 1600 processes) bigger. This behavior implies that the static configuration using 10 navigators and 22 dispatchers is more suitable to run the workload. Thus, configuring the system manually and statically potentially leads to a suboptimal configuration both in terms of performance and resource allocation. The *static 22/10* configuration serves as a good example for this behavior: while it is between 10% and 62% faster than the autonomic strategies tested, it also uses the most resources (between 108% and 262%more).

As shown in Figure 9.5b, the *simple* optimization strategy slowly grows the system to its maximum size keeping the number of dispatchers and navigators balanced, which turns out to be a sub-optimal configuration. This leads to an excessive use of the resources, although the high allocation does not enhance the performance. The time required to execute the 800 processes batch using the simple optimization strategy is 22% higher than in case of the *static 22/10* configuration. The two main reasons for this behavior are the following. First, the simple optimization strategy adapts slowly to the workload imposed on the system. In the case of 800 processes it requires 24.49 seconds to grow to the full configuration because it adds only 1 node at a time.

The other reason is the suboptimal partitioning of the nodes between navigators and dispatchers. This can also be seen in Figure 9.6. This figure illustrates the evolution of the configuration along its two main dimensions (the number of navigators and the number of dispatchers) when using different strategies. While the *static 22/10* configuration performs better and the inverse configuration (22 navigators, 10 dispatchers) performs worse, the *simple* optimization strategy converges to an intermediate configuration (17n, 15d) because both space sizes exceed the thresholds, letting the configuration grow symmetrically until saturation is reached. All other optimization strategies tend towards the former with (8n, 22d) for the *differential* optimization strategy and (12n, 20d) for the *proportional* optimization strategy.

The *differential* optimization strategy performs better (13% in the case of 800 processes batch) than the *simple* optimization strategy regarding time and has up to 39% (400 processes batch) smaller allocation than all other strategies. The reason why the execution of the same workload takes up to 62% longer than the *static 22/10* configura-

9. Basic Policies

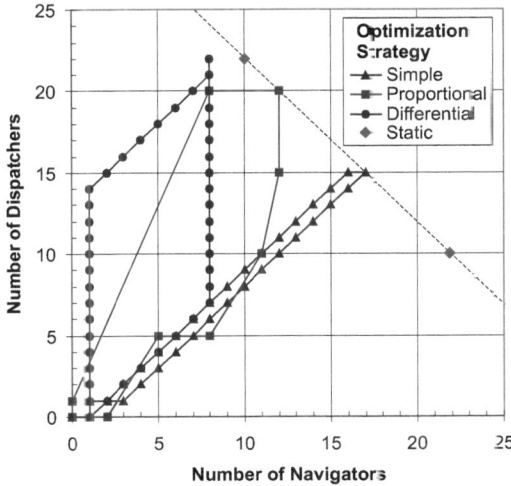

Figure 9.6.: Configurations reached by different optimization strategies

tion is found in its slow adaptation to the workload, similar to the *simple* strategies. In contrast to the *simple* optimization strategy, the *differential* optimization strategy only increases the number of threads as long as the space growth is bigger than the thresholds T_{start}^d or T_{start}^n: as soon as the process space stops growing (8n, 7d in Figure 9.6 or after 10s in Figure 9.5c), the number of navigators remains the same whereas the number of dispatchers is still increasing according to the growth of the task space. This slow and also resource saving way of growing the configuration is the main reason why the allocation is generally low; this optimization strategy does not saturate the system like the *simple* optimization strategy, but rather devotes only the strictly necessary nodes.

The *proportional* optimization strategy performs only slightly worse with regard to the batch time than the *static 22/10* configuration, but does better in terms of allocation. The difference in time can be explained with the delay required to grow the configuration: while this is none in case of the static configuration, it takes 14.56 seconds to reach the full configuration in case of the *proportional* optimization strategy, increasing the overall batch execution time by a maximum of 18%.

Regarding the resource allocation, the result of this optimization strategy compared to the static configuration is only little lower when executing the 1600 processes batch and significantly lower when executing the 400 processes batch. This result indicates that the controller adapts to the size of the workload. In case of 1600 processes, the controller grows the configuration until all nodes are used whereas in the case of 400 processes only part of the nodes will be used.

9.3. Conclusions

Using the simple optimization strategy of monitoring the size of process and task space in order to determine reconfiguration actions, has already led to very promising results. As expected however, it is difficult to determine a globally optimal optimization strategy. The strategies we evaluated offer different characteristics along the trade-off between execution time and resource allocation. Thus, a strategy can be chosen to drive the automatic configuration of the system according to the overall goal within this trade-off.

Although the optimization strategies we introduced already performed satisfactorily, we intend to further extend them. For example, the random selection strategy employed here works well in homogeneous environments, but may need a more refined model of the configuration and more advanced selection strategies to deal with heterogeneous environments. Similarly, the information strategy we introduced is based on the current state of the system. It would be useful to enhance it by taking into account the history of the system's configuration and past performance.

Each optimization strategy can also be tuned by setting its threshold parameters. In the experiments, we did so heuristically by observing the behavior of the system and estimating the capacity of each type of thread. In general, setting these thresholds appropriately tends to be difficult and misconfiguring them may also result in a performance penalty.

In this chapter we have presented a first set of policies with which we have configured the behavior of the autonomic controller. For each of the policies, we have used uniform information and selection strategies and have implemented and tested different optimization strategies. As our performance evaluation with different workload sizes indicates, the controller outperformed the manual, static configuration by achieving a good tradeoff between two different goals: minimizing resource allocation while guaranteeing satisfying performance. All optimization strategies presented however still require thresholds which have to be manually configured. Such configuration is very difficult and requires in depth knowledge of the system at hand and also depends on the workloads being executed. We will address the problem of removing such thresholds in the next chapter.

10. Zero Configuration Policies

As has been shown in the previous chapter, the behavior of the autonomic controller can be defined using policies. Approaches which are based on thresholds however tend to tune the controller for a specific workload. In this chapter we present two new policies, gradually working toward the goal of zero-configuration policies. With this we want to detach the policy completely from the workload but will still adapt the configuration on the fly to suit the current workload. To do so, we first present a PID controller policy in Section 10.1, a well-known concept from the literature and from applications in the industry. The PID controller however still requires configuration and we thus move on to develop a policy (Section 10.2) more tightly coupled to the system. The balancing policy is derived from an analytical view of the system and depends only on parameters which can be measured and set at runtime. We compare these two new policies with an extensive set of measurements in Section 10.3 and draw conclusions in Section 10.4.

10.1. PID Controller Policy

A PID controller [53] is a common feedback loop used in many traditional industrial control systems. As shown in Figure 10.1, it maps the control error ($e(t)$), which measures how far is the system from the reference input) to a control action that aims at correcting such error. To do so, it combines three terms: proportional, integral, and derivative, each having its own weight (or gain).

$$c(t) = c_p e(t) + c_i \int_0^t e(\tau)d\tau + c_d \frac{de(t)}{dt} \qquad (10.1)$$

The proportional part corrects the current error, the integral part compensates for the steady state error (if $e(t) = 0$) and the derivative part helps to avoid oscillations.

To apply the PID controller to the JOpera engine, we need to define the control error in terms of the engine's performance and define the control actions in terms of which reconfiguration actions are available.

Since we are interested in removing all external dependencies of the controller, we choose not to rely on an external input defining the set-point of the system (which would have to be adjusted by system administrators). Instead, we rely on a combination of internal observable parameters (i.e., the size of the spaces) only.

Based on the intuition that the system is ideally configured if its spaces are of equal size, we combine the measurements of the space sizes as follows:

$$E(t) = \frac{s_{Process}(t) + s_{Event}(t)}{s_{Task}(t)} \qquad (10.2)$$

10. Zero Configuration Policies

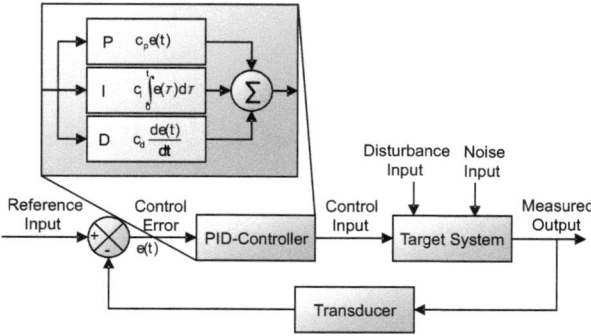

Figure 10.1.: Feedback control loop with PID controller

where $s_{Space}(t)$ is the current space size. For $s_{Task}(t) = 0$ we set $E(t) = \infty$.

Since $E(t) > 0$, it is not suitable to be used as direct input to the PID controller. We thus normalize it:

$$e(t) = \begin{cases} E(t) - 1 & E(t) \geq 1 \\ 1 - \frac{1}{E(t)} & 0 < E(t) < 1 \end{cases} \qquad (10.3)$$

With this definition of the control error, the system is balanced if $s_{Process}(t) + s_{Event}(t) = s_{Task}(t) \Rightarrow e(t) = 0$ and thus, no reconfiguration action should occur. Because in this case the control input is zero (as no change in the configuration is required), the steady state error is zero as well and the integral term can therefore be dropped ($c_i = 0$) from the PID controller.

Likewise, we can define what reconfiguration action should be taken. If $s_{Process}(t) + s_{Event}(t) < s_{Task}(t) \Rightarrow e(t) < 0$, more dispatchers should be added, as the task space is bigger. If $e(t) > 0$ we are in the opposite situation, and more navigators (and less dispatchers) are required. The resulting abstract control error in the interval of $[-\infty, \infty]$ is then mapped by the selection strategy to an actual reconfiguration in the interval bounded by $[0, a]$, where a is the total number of nodes available in the cluster.

The resulting PID controller still needs to be tuned, by setting appropriate values to the gains of the proportional c_p and derivative c_d terms. The advantage of choosing a standard controller is that the problem of tuning its parameter is well understood [127] and several heuristics are available [25]. Some of these however require to subject the system to controlled input waveforms and cannot always be applied to tune a system in production which may be subject to unpredictable workloads. The resulting PID controller is also not robust with respect to changes in the workload, and thus has to be repeatedly tuned. Moreover, to rely on a PID controller with a single control error input we had to combine multiple measurements of the system's performance in a somewhat arbitrary way. Using a Multiple-Input Multiple-Output PID controller would have made its automatic tuning more difficult [71]. We expect to obtain better results with a controller that is based on a model more tightly coupled to the architecture of the system under control

10.2. Balancing (Zero-Configuration) Policy

The goal for this policy is to go beyond the fairly basic approach used by the policies presented in Chapter 9 and the very general solution of the PID Controller as discussed in Section 10.1. This policy uses an analytical model which is more tightly coupled to the characteristics of the system and which, as the PID controller policy does, refrains from using thresholds.

This policy is referred to as the *Balancing policy* as it tries to balance the consumers and producers of the spaces based on the rate at which messages are written and read from them.

Figure 10.2 shows a summary of the produced and consumed messages. A navigator takes r_n messages per second from the event space. Each message is processed and, depending on the structure of the workflow being executed, a task execution request may be written to the task space with the probability c_1. Therefore – assuming that all navigators work at the same rate – in one second n navigators take nr_n messages from the event space and enqueue $c_1 n r_n$ tasks into the task space. External process execution requests get into the system via the process space with rate e.

On the other side of the spaces, a dispatcher takes r_d task execution request messages per second from the task space, sends for each executed task c_2 messages back into the event space. Therefore – again, assuming a uniform task execution speed – d dispatchers get dr_d tasks from the task space and write $c_2 d r_d$ events every second to the event space.

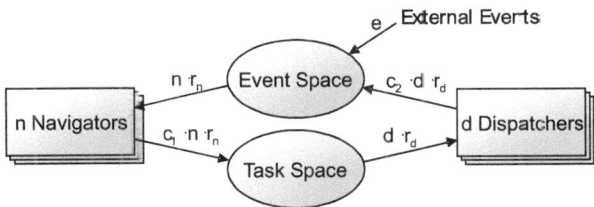

Figure 10.2.: Modeling Communication Flows through the Spaces

The space growth is the difference of the rate at which messages are put into the space and are taken out of it. We define p as the total number of messages in the spaces consumed by the navigators (the event and process space) and q as the number of messages in the task space, consumed by the dispatchers. Hence the growth of the spaces (p' and q') can be defined as follows, taking into account the number of messages that are written and read from a space per unit of time.

$$p' = c_2 dr_d + e - nr_n \qquad (10.4)$$
$$q' = c_1 nr_n - dr_d \qquad (10.5)$$

Following the same strategy as with the PID controller, the goal of this policy is also to ensure equal space growth, so that $p' = q'$:

$$(c_2 + 1)dr_d + e = (c_1 + 1)nr_n \qquad (10.6)$$

We resolve (10.6) with respect to n:

$$n_{opt} = \frac{(c_2 + 1)dr_d + e}{(c_1 + 1)r_n} \qquad (10.7)$$

This equation represents how many navigators (n_{opt}) are needed in order to obtain the balanced state $p' = q'$.

If we express the number of dispatchers d as the difference between the number of available nodes in the cluster a and the number of navigators n, we can substitute $d = a - n$ and can define the balanced configuration as a function of measurable variables:

$$n_{opt} = \frac{(c_2 + 1)ar_d + e}{(c_2 + 1)r_d + (c_1 + 1)r_n} \qquad (10.8)$$

In order to calculate (10.8), the controller continuously averages the execution rates of navigators and dispatchers to arrive at r_d, r_n, measures e from the process space and uses a from the current configuration of the cluster. The values of the two parameters c_1, c_2 are calculated by solving (10.5) and (10.4):

$$c_1 = \frac{q' + dr_d}{nr_n} \qquad (10.9)$$
$$c_2 = \frac{p' + nr_n - e}{dr_d} \qquad (10.10)$$

and by additionally measuring the growth in both spaces (p', q').

As opposed to the information fed into the PID controller, the balancing policy depends on more information (i.e., the rates e, r_d, r_n, p', q') but does not require any manual tuning.

In order to prevent the system from behaving erratically at startup, the values of the parameters c_1, c_2 can be initialized by analyzing the communication protocol between the dispatcher and navigator. The constant c_2 is the number of messages sent by the dispatcher into the event space during the execution of a task. By design $c_2 = 4$, as the dispatcher goes through four different states during task execution and sends a notification for each state transition. The constant c_1 is defined as the probability the navigator sends a message into the task space when it processes an incoming message. This depends on the structure of the workflow being executed. However, in general, for a workflow of t tasks, the navigator will receive $4t$ events from the dispatcher, one from the API and 5 from the state changes of the process executed. Thus:

$$c_1 = \frac{t}{4t+6} \qquad (10.11)$$

Since a process contains at least one task[1] ($t = 1$), the lower bound of c_1 is $\frac{1}{10}$. For the upper bound:

$$\lim_{t \to \infty} \frac{t}{4t+6} = \frac{1}{4} \qquad (10.12)$$

From this analysis, the initial value of c_1 should be bound to the interval $[\frac{1}{10}, \frac{1}{4}[$.

To validate this analysis we have measured the values of the two constants using a heterogeneous set of workflow patterns. Figures 10.3(a) and 10.3(b) show that the observed values of the parameters are consistent with the analysis across a representative set of workflows. As an interesting result, the standard deviation of c_1 for workloads with parallel processes are much higher than for other workloads. This is caused by the uneven distribution of tasks written to the task space during process execution: All tasks of a parallel process are written to the space at the beginning of the process and none thereafter.

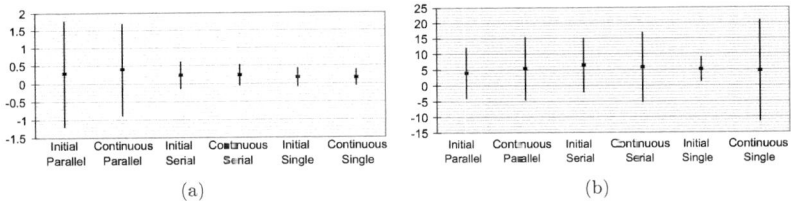

Figure 10.3.: Measuring c_1 (a) & c_2 (b) over a representative set of workloads

10.3. Evaluation

In this section we evaluate the performance of the autonomic workflow engine with a controller that uses the policies presented in Sections 10.1 and 10.2. We analyze the behavior of the Balancing policy and the PID Controller policy for three different workloads. We compare the workload execution durations for the different policies, including – as a baseline – the proportional optimization policy (Section 9.1 of the previous chapter) that requires manual setting of the thresholds.

---
[1]There can also be empty processes, but they do not need the dispatcher to run

10. Zero Configuration Policies

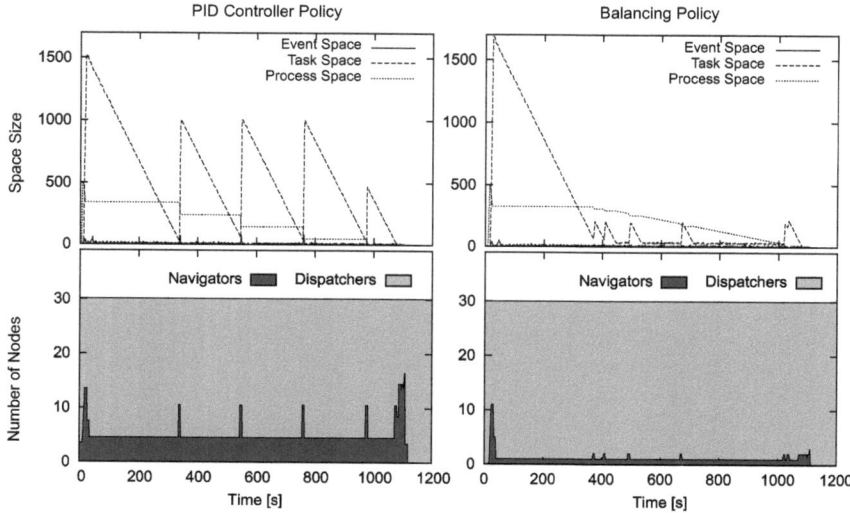

Figure 10.4.: Busy Workload Execution Plots

10.3.1. Experimental Setup

The experiments to evaluate the two policies were carried out using two clusters. The first cluster consists of 30 1GHz dual P-III with 1GB memory, running Sun's Java Development Kit version 1.5.09 on Linux kernel version 2.4.22. The second cluster consists of six 1.4GHz dual AMD Athlon with 1GB memory, running JDK version 1.5.09 on Linux kernel version 2.6.8. The autonomic controller was run on an additional dedicated node.

10.3.2. Busy Workload

The busy workload consists of 500 workflows, each executing in parallel 10 CPU intensive tasks performing number primality tests for an execution time of 10 seconds. All workflows are started at the beginning of the benchmark. Because of the resource consumption and long duration of the tasks, we expect this workload to saturate all available nodes of the cluster and thus require as many dispatchers as possible to execute the tasks.

Figure 10.4 shows the execution plots for the Balancing policy and the PID Controller policy. The upper charts show the evolution of the process, event and task space, while the lower charts show the evolution of the configuration consisting of the number of navigators and dispatchers allocated.

10. Zero Configuration Policies

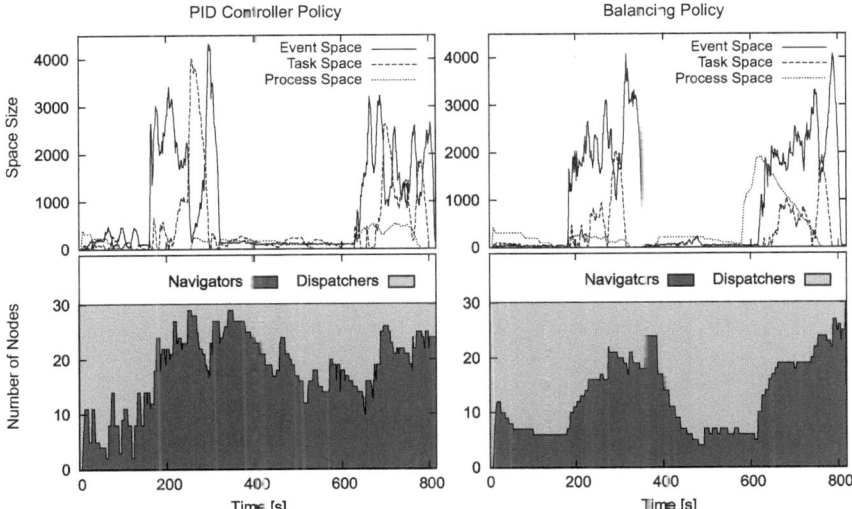

Figure 10.5.: Burst Workload Execution Plots

The PID Controller policy adapts quickly to the growing task space and allocates a maximum of 29 dispatchers for the whole execution duration. Once the task space is nearly empty, the control error will lead the controller to start a number of navigators. These additional navigators will quickly fill up the task space due to the structure of the workflows having 10 parallel initial tasks. The growth of the task space will cause the controller to increase the number of dispatchers. This pattern is repeated several times, letting the configuration oscillate until the workload is processed completely.

The Balancing policy behaves very similar to the PID Controller policy in that it assigns most nodes of the cluster to run dispatchers. In contrast to the PID controller it avoids oscillations, resulting in a much smoother evolution of the configuration. The stability of the configuration also results in a steady decrease of the process space size.

10.3.3. Burst Workload

The motivation of this workload is to test whether the autonomic controller can reconfigure the system as the characteristics of the workload change. The workload starts with a burst of 500 processes which execute a sequence of 10 CPU intensive tasks lasting 1 second. As soon as 95% of the processes terminate, the second burst is started. It consists of 2000 processes of 10 parallel empty tasks with a duration approximately 0s.

10. Zero Configuration Policies

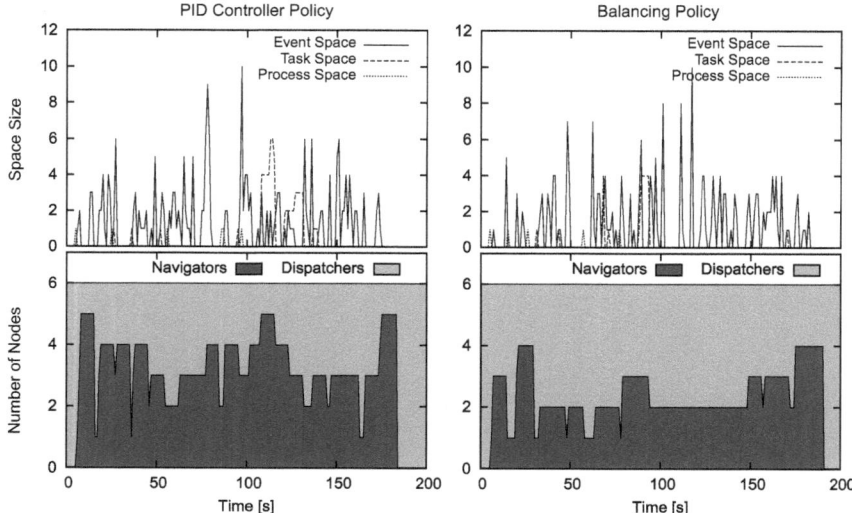

Figure 10.6.: fMRI Workload Execution Plots

Again, as soon as 95% of the processes have finished, a third burst is started similar to the first one. The fourth burst has the same characteristics as the second.

We expect an approximation of the following configuration evolution for this experiment. When bursts 2 & 4, each containing ten tasks to be executed in parallel are fed into the system, the task space will grow very fast. As the tasks however can be executed in virtually no time, not many dispatchers will be required. The event space will soon after also start to grow very fast. This is due to the many events that are generated for the quickly executed tasks. Because of the proportionally big event space, the controller is likely to allocate more navigators. In contrast to this, the task space will not grow nearly as quickly in case of bursts 1 & 3. In fact, the task space is expected to grow shortly and then to maintain the size (as for each task taken from it, a new task will be enqueued as the tasks are executed serially). After each burst we expect the controller to slowly increase the number of dispatchers as this type of workload requires more dispatchers. The evolution of the space sizes described before can be observed in Figure 10.5.

The PID Controller policy does not completely follow the expected reconfigurations. It starts with about 20 dispatchers in order to cope with the more CPU intense workload. At second 170, after the second burst has been started, it starts to allocate more navigators. The reconfiguration required for the third burst however is not completely carried out. The controller allocates roughly equal numbers of navigators and dispatchers. The configuration change for the fourth burst again is as expected as more navigators are allocated.

The Balancing policy behaves according to the expectations outlined before by allocating a large number of dispatchers at the first and the second burst. For the second burst the number of navigators is increased but the configuration is unstable. It seems to be much harder to get a stable configuration for processes with longer and busier tasks than with short idle tasks. The reason for this is the high execution rate of the navigators. A navigator is able to handle up to 200 events per second. Stopping or starting just one navigator results in a big change in the event space growth which then leads to a very varying input for the policy. The fourth burst finally is handled by using about 20 navigators.

Besides a difference in the reconfiguration decisions taken in response to the bursts, the Balancing policy also seems to maintain a much more stable configuration throughout the experiment. In contrast, the controller performs many more reconfigurations and does not get into a stable state in case of the PID Controller policy. Moreover, the configuration seems to oscillate at times, for instance during the execution of the first burst. This oscillation is due to the parameter setting of the PID controller for this specific type of workload. The parameters are set once and are used for all workloads. It clearly is not possible to choose these values so that they fit for all types of workloads. During the whole course of the experiment, the PID Controller policy requires twice as many reconfigurations than the Balancing policy does, performing approximately 200 reconfigurations

10.3.4. fMRI Workload

The processes of this workload are used in real experiments in the field of Functional Magnetic Resonance Imaging (fMRI)[54]. Such a process is used to process raw data of brain scans and takes in a first step the raw data, aligns it to a reference brain image by reslicing it, averages over several scans executed with different wavelengths, and finally slices along the x, y and z dimensions. The structure is simple with two phases of parallel program executions as depicted in Figure 10.7.

The workload consists of ten fMRI processes which are started one after the other with a delay of 10s. The challenge of this workload is that the processes contain relatively long executing tasks (up to twenty seconds). As the workload consists only of few processes started continuously one after the other, the spaces are virtually empty for most of the time (see plots in Figure 13.13). This makes it very difficult for a policy observing space sizes to select an appropriate configuration.

The PID Controller policy reacts to this challenging workload with many reconfigurations. As the task space is mostly empty and the event space shows few peaks only, this policy assigns on average slightly more navigators than dispatchers. A spike in the event space is usually followed by an allocation of an increased number of navigators. Again in case of this workload, the PID Controller policy seems unable to maintain a stable configuration, letting the configuration oscillate slightly.

10. Zero Configuration Policies

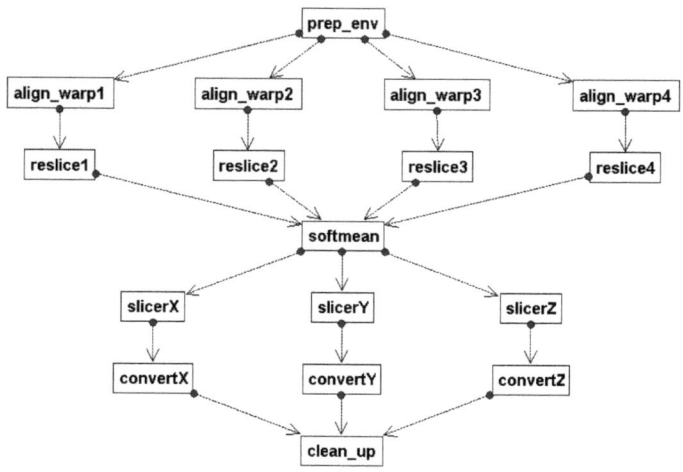

Figure 10.7.: Structure of the fMRI process

The Balancing policy behaves better than the PID Controller policy and on average uses two dispatchers more, which seems reasonable in face of the computationally very intense tasks. This policy also leads to fewer reconfigurations (about 20 compared to 40 reconfigurations for the PID Controller policy as Figure 10.9 shows).

10.3.5. Comparison

Figure 10.8 shows the execution durations of the three workloads using the Proportional optimization policy, the PID Controller policy and the Balancing policy. For the Proportional optimization policy, the best known threshold settings (10/5) have been used.

As the qualitative analysis already has pointed out, the PID Controller policy and the balancing policy are about equally fast (average of 1103.5s and 1098.3s) for the Busy Workload, but more than 40% faster than the proportional optimization policy (1920s). The proportional optimization policy does not assign as many dispatchers as the other two policies do and hence requires more time to execute the workload.

For the Burst Workload the improvement is not as explicit, but still 20% for the Balancing policy (738.45s) and 9% for the PID Controller policy (837.88s) compared to the Proportional optimization policy (917.98s). This is still a good result, even if the qualitative analysis has shown that improvements are still possible. If we change the constants of the Proportional optimization policy, we are able to push down the execution time to the value of the PID Controller, but we lose about 20% performance

10. Zero Configuration Policies

in case of the Busy Workload, illustrating again that thresholds are geared toward specific workloads.

In case of the fMRI Workload, we have about the same performance gain than for the Burst Workload. The Balancing policy (177.5s) is 22% faster than the Proportional optimization policy (226.3s) and the PID Controller policy has a gain of 8% (208.9s).

In order to highlight the differences between the PID Controller and the Balancing policy, which processed the workloads similarly fast, Figure 10.9 shows the number of reconfigurations required for the two policies. In case of all workloads, the Balancing policy performs fewer reconfigurations, indicating that in this case the configuration oscillates less during the course of an experiment.

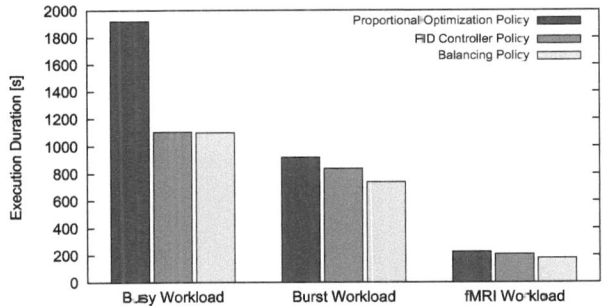

Figure 10.8.: Performance Comparison

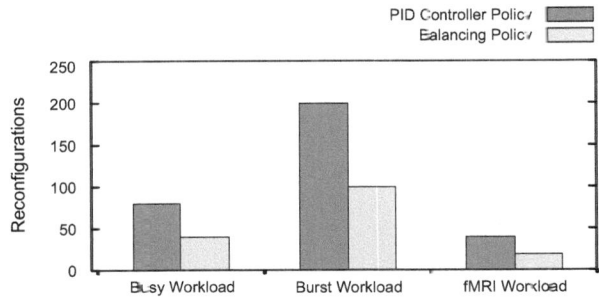

Figure 10.9.: Number of Reconfigurations

10.4. Conclusions

Many autonomic systems achieve self-configuration through a controller component, which monitors a system's operations as well as performance and reacts to imbalances due to workload changes by applying reconfiguration actions. Whereas employing such a controller can remove the need for manual system configuration, most simple controllers depend on thresholds and if-then rules, whose parameters still require tuning as has been shown in Chapter 9. Manual configuration of an autonomic controller however defeats the purpose of self-configuration and we have therefore presented two zero-configuration control policies, the first based on a standardized PID controller, for which an extensive literature on tuning techniques is available. The second is based on an analytical model applicable to stage-based architectures, where the controller ensures that the rate of message production and consumption through a space remains balanced. This policy can self-tune its operating parameters based on observable properties of the system and thus requires zero-configuration. The evaluation in the context to the JOpera autonomic workflow engine has shown the feasibility of using zero-configuration policies for realistic workloads. Not only the proposed policies do not require any manual configuration, but they provide a significant performance gain over simpler policies based on thresholds, even when these are optimally tuned.

11. Conclusions

In this part of the book we have first presented the architecture of JOpera and how its functionality can be replicated across a cluster. We have demonstrated the difficulty of configuring the distributed execution engine and have with this motivated the need for adding self-configuration capabilities to the engine. With the added autonomic controller the engine can automatically reconfigure itself based on the current workload by using autonomic computing techniques. This is an important contribution, as workflow management systems are being more and more applied to domains that can be characterized by the unpredictability of their workloads, such as – for instance – process-based orchestration of Web services. In the past, distribution has been applied to the design of many workflow engines in order to improve their scalability and reliability. However, very little attention has been paid to the need for properly configuring such distributed systems. This, in practice, remains a difficult, error-prone, manual and time-consuming operation, especially when deploying the system to face an unpredictable workload.

We have therefore shown how to apply the autonomic computing paradigm to greatly simplify the deployment and the maintenance of such systems. As our experiments indicate the autonomic controller of JOpera can adapt the system configuration optimally to unforeseeable, changing workload characteristics. The system furthermore takes failures into account and adapts the system's configuration accordingly. Although the results presented were obtained with relatively homogeneous workloads, we will explore the effects of workloads with more complex characteristics as part of future work as the system is deployed in realistic production settings.

We have further presented a first set of policies which were used to define the behavior of the autonomic controller. At the core of these polices is the definition of the optimization strategy. The different optimization strategies we presented have been able to grow and shrink the number of threads in response to surges in the workload. Also, if the all resources of the engine, all nodes in the assigned cluster were in use, the autonomic controller would balance the number of dispatchers and navigators, thereby not just reacting to the surge itself, but also to the characteristics of the workload. As the measurements have shown, the autonomic controller configured even with basic policies outperforms manual configuration in our experiments.

However, all optimization strategies presented still require manual configuration by setting thresholds which is far from being trivial. We have therefore tried to remove any need for configuration from the autonomic controller. In a first step we implemented a policy which at its core features a PID controller. PID controllers are well studied and literature for properly tuning them is available. The PID controller policy however still requires the setting of parameters and we have in a next step developed a balancing policy which tries to ensure that the rate of messages production and consumption by the

11. Conclusions

dispatchers and navigators exchanged through the spaces remains balanced. This policy can self-tune its operating parameters based on observable properties of the system and thus requires zero-configuration. Both policies provide a significant performance gain over the basic policies.

Part III.
Data Lineage Tracking

12. Data Lineage Tracking

12.1. Introduction

Data lineage and data provenance have been identified as a major problem in the management of scientific data. The problem has become more acute as scientists increasingly use computational means to produce derived data sets [13, 16, 17, 27, 80, 102, 118].

Without lineage information, a data set is often useless from a scientific point of view. The question is then how to capture the lineage information of a data set, how to store it efficiently, and how to allow queries over it. The first part of the problem, capturing the lineage information, has been made substantially easier by the widespread use of workflow tools to describe scientific computations [7, 86, 88, 108]. The workflow process describes what steps were used to produce a particular data set and, hence, can be used to trace the lineage of it. Unfortunately, there are no efficient ways to store and query workflow based lineage information. Existing proposals, e.g., Trio [4] and GridDB [70] use recursive queries to retrieve the lineage of a data set. Such an approach does neither scale for large workflow processes nor for large collections of data sets.

From our experience working with scientists in biology [5] and astrophysics [106, 107], it is clear that obtaining the basic lineage is not enough. Scientists are interested in answering queries such as "What algorithms were used to derive this data set?", "Which data sets have been produced with this algorithm?", "What data sets have been derived from this data set?", and so on. While these queries are related to the basic lineage information, being able to answer all of them efficiently requires to have an efficient way to store and query the provenance of every data set.

In this part of the book we first show that existing approaches which use recursive queries to store lineage information do not scale. We therefore want to find approaches which scale better. For this we first show that workflows with a tree structure produce lineage dependencies that can be very efficiently stored and queried using interval encoding [63]. We then analyze the problem of encoding general workflow graphs by characterizing the problem and showing that the number of dimensions for the encoding depends on the structure of the graph. This makes it impossible to use a single encoding for arbitrary graphs. However, we need to use a single encoding to be able to store the information in a relational database. Thus, we then proceed to explore the problem of transforming arbitrary workflow graphs into tree-like graphs amenable to interval encoding [47].

With this, the interval encoding for DAGs (IDAG) presented here can encode arbitrary DAGs with intervals. We provide the transformation algorithms, discuss how to optimize the transformation procedure, and present an extensive collection of experiments that evaluate IDAG using random graphs and a set of representative scientific workflows. The experiments show that IDAG is more efficient than the recursive techniques.

Having presented IDAG, we move on to evaluate the viability of using it to store the lineage data produced by processing raw biological experiment data using workflows. However, from the point of view of a biologist, the lineage information provided by such automated processing pipelines is often obvious and too coarse-grained. In most cases, it is just a correlation between processing modules and input/output data files. Such information is often only of limited value, especially when the input and output files contain multiple data items.

Collecting fine-grained lineage by correlating data items in the different processed files is what allows users of the processing pipelines to ask more detailed and interesting lineage questions. Unlike lineage tracking in databases or lineage from non-automated processing workflows, automated processing pipelines pose difficult challenges in terms of efficiently storing and managing lineage information. When capturing and managing such fine-grained lineage, the amount of data and the complexity of the interdependencies is often much larger than in other settings.

We show how to address these problems by describing the algorithms and lineage management strategies implemented in Sisyphus, a tool supporting a real data processing pipeline from the proteomics domain. We first discuss the biological background as well as the data processing pipeline and show how fine-grained data lineage can be extracted from it. It is particularly the fine-grained lineage which has a very complex and intricate structure making storing and retrieving it efficiently a challenge. Different encodings are necessary to account for both simple dependencies that can be captured in the form of a tree and complex, DAG like dependencies that need more sophisticated approaches. We discuss different encodings already described in the literature, GRIPP [111], Dual [120] as well as IDAG and the recursive approach both of which have been discussed in the previous chapter. We provide several optimizations to these encodings and, using the original code provided by the authors, perform an exhaustive cost analysis using real lineage data from a proteomics experiments. Our experiments show that there is a non-trivial trade-off between storage space and query response time. Nevertheless, the results indicate that an improved version of IDAG seems to be the one offering the best performance for our application. We have implemented the best strategy in Sisyphus.

The remainder of this part of the book is structured as follows. The rest of this chapter discusses related work.

In Chapter 13 we map the problem of tracking & storing workflow lineage on the problem of storing and retrieving DAGs in relational DBMSs. We discuss the limited scalability of current solutions and develop the IDAG approach used to transform arbitrary graphs, making them amenable for interval encoding. The evaluation of the approach shows that it allows for significant faster retrieval than current approaches use to store lineage information.

Following this, in Chapter 14, we put the IDAG approach to use for a concrete application. It is being used for storing the fine-grained lineage information of processed biological experiment data in Sisyphus. We present the biological background of the project and discuss the structure of the lineage information. Graph reachability approaches are also used for storing and retrieving lineage information and we compare them to IDAG in a thorough evaluation.

Conclusions are drawn in Chapter 15.

12.2. Related Work

A number of systems to capture and manage the data lineage from workflow executions has been developed. These systems do however only address the problem of capturing and storing coarse-grained lineage from workflow executions and focus on other lineage related challenges. Consequently, very little work has been done on efficiently storing and querying large amounts of lineage information.

The Trio [4] system is an extension of relational databases to support uncertainty and lineage. It bases lineage storage on methods described in [11] by storing the lineage information in additional tables. Retrieving the lineage information is then done as described in [28] using recursive queries.

The GridDB [70] system provides the user with the means to process data in a database similar to a workflow system, also tracking the lineage. It provides the user with a declarative interface to apply transformations to data. Lineage information is stored during the execution in the same tables as are the files registered in the system.

Zoom [12] aims at providing users with the ability to define user views over workflow lineage. Such views allow to collapse sub-workflows in the lineage in order to reduce the complexity and disentangle the graphical representation.

The PASOA [79] project targets at collecting lineage information from provenance-aware distributed service in a service oriented architecture environment.

GridDB, Zoom and PASOA use recursive queries to retrieve the lineage information and thus suffers from the scalability limitations discussed in this paper.

The Karma framework [103] is designed to capture the lineage of data sent and received from services orchestrated using a workflow and also collects lineage information of the workflow execution similar to PASOA.

The challenge of managing and visualizing large amounts of lineage data is addressed by VisTrails [18]. This system provides users with a visual workbench to design and execute workflows and more importantly to visually explore the lineage of the execution.

Karma and VisTrais only allow to retrieve an entire lineage graph at a time in order to visualize it but do not allow for more detailed queries.

None of the systems discussed before has addressed the problem of fine-grained lineage and consequently none faces similar efficiency problems when storing big lineage graphs.

13. Efficient Lineage Storage

Before presenting IDAG, we first study the problem of storing the transitive closure of directed acyclic graphs in relational DBMSs (Section 13.1). We compare two different approaches to do so and highlight their limited scalability with respect to retrieval time or storage space required, motivating the use of interval encoding instead. We then show the limited applicability of this approach for arbitrary DAGs (Section 13.2) and discuss how to transform arbitrary graphs into interval encodable graphs (Section 13.3). The approach is evaluated in Section 13.4.

13.1. Workflow Based Data Lineage

13.1.1. Workflow Model

Workflows are widely used in scientific applications [10, 23, 54, 72, 96, 99, 104]. Workflows orchestrate the execution of tasks by means of a graph that defines the control and data flow between those tasks. A workflow takes a collection of data sets as input and produces a collection of data sets as output. The tasks also take data sets as input and produce data sets as output. The dependencies between tasks and data sets are determined by the control and data flow described as part of the workflow process. Therefore, the lineage of a data set can be determined by tracing back how it was produced using the corresponding workflow.

For the purposes of this paper we treat workflows as directed acyclic graphs (DAGs). Although some workflow tools allow cycles, any execution of a workflow process can be represented as a DAG by unrolling the loops. In this paper we assume that this is always the case. The nodes of the DAG represent tasks and data sets. The edges represent dependencies between them. A directed edge will point from a task to a data set if it the data set is an output of the task, and from a data set to a task if the data set is used as input to the task. This completely captures all dependencies between tasks and data sets, and between data sets and data sets.

The lineage information induced by the DAG is the transitive closure of all dependencies. Hence, from here on we treat the problem of storing and querying the lineage information as the problem of storing and querying the transitive closure of the dependency graph.

For the experimental setup used in the remainder of this section please refer to Section 13.4. Deviations from this setup are explained in the text.

13.1.2. Lineage Using Recursive Queries

Systems like Trio and GridDB use recursive queries to retrieve lineage information. The dependencies between data sets are stored using a relation with two attributes of the form Dependency(parent_id, child_id). To find the lineage of a data set, the query recursively asks for the parents of the data set, the parents of the parents, and so on.

We have assessed the performance of this approach by measuring the time it takes to retrieve the lineage of a leaf node of a randomly generated DAG (between 5 and 100 nodes and random edges). The experiments were carried out using a Postgres DBMS and, because of the lack for support for recursive queries, stored procedures querying the relations recursively were used. The results are shown in Figure 13.1(a), where the time to obtain the lineage information is plotted against the number of nodes in the dependency graph.

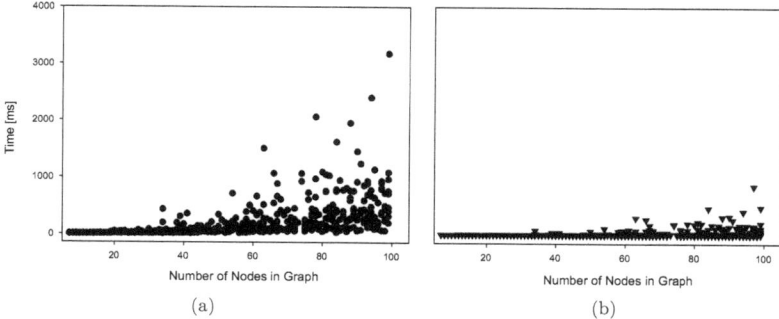

Figure 13.1.: Response time for (a) recursive queries and (b) queries over all paths for random graphs.

The time it takes to execute recursive queries is linear with the number of paths in the graph. For small graphs, with less than 30 nodes, the response time grows slowly. Beyond 30 nodes, however, the query time becomes unpredictable, growing exponentially high - in some cases up to 3 seconds per query. This behavior, combined with the linear growth in query time with the number of paths in the graph, makes recursive queries unsuitable for exploring the lineage of large scientific workflows.

13.1.3. Lineage Using All Paths

Recursive queries minimize the amount of information to store at the cost of longer query running times. The other extreme would be to trade space for speed and store all paths in the DAG so that the query only needs to retrieve the corresponding paths. Finding

13. Efficient Lineage Storage

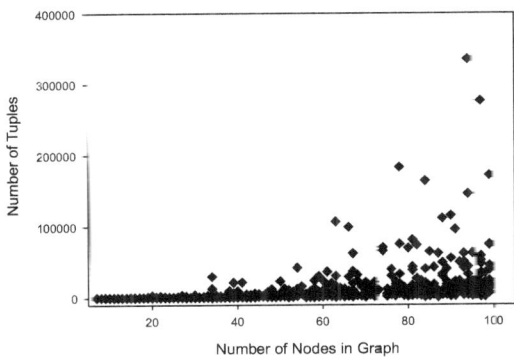

Figure 13.2.: Storage space required for the all paths approach.

all paths in a directed acyclic graph amounts to topologically sorting the graph. This can be done in linear time or, more precisely, for a graph $G = (V, E)$, in $O(|V| + |E|)$. A topological sort of the graph will yield all total orders, which is equivalent to all paths P through the graph. This can be done offline and needs to be done only once for every workflow, so the cost is amortized over time. An efficient way of storing all paths is based on the observation that since the path p_i is a total order, each element/data set $e \in p_i$ for $p_i \in F$ can be assigned an integer denoting the position o on p_i. The triples e, i and o are stored in a relation Paths(path_id, node_id, order_no). The query to retrieve the lineage of a data set given the data set ID nid is as follows:

```
SELECT pt2.node_id
  FROM Paths pt1, Paths pt2
 WHERE pt1.node_id = nid AND
       pt1.path_id = pt2.path_id AND
       pt1.order_no > pt2.order_no
```

The query selects all the paths that contain a given node n, retrieves all the nodes found on those paths and filters over the order, such that only elements occurring before n on those paths are returned.

We evaluate the performance of this approach using a collection of random DAGs. The results are shown in Figure 13.1(b) where the time to obtain the lineage information is plotted against the number of nodes in the dependency graph. As the figure shows, the path approach scales better than recursive queries. However, in Figure 13.2 we show the number of tuples required to store all paths against the number of nodes in the graph. Storing all paths may lead to a large storage overhead. If several thousand workflow executions need to be stored, these large numbers can become problematic by degrading performance.

13.1.4. Lineage Over Interval Tree Encoding

The results of these initial experiments indicate that the two techniques examined represent two extremes. Recursive queries require little space but can be very slow. Storing all paths leads to faster queries but the storage requirements grow too large. Clearly, an alternative is needed. Encoding the transitive closure of a tree to store it in a database and retrieve it efficiently has already been used in several applications [32, 81, 112] with the basic idea stemming from [63]. The approach uses one-dimensional intervals over the natural numbers to represent nodes in the tree. If a node n_1 is a predecessor of another node n_2, the interval representing n_1 must enclose the interval representing n_2. More formally, a node n_i is represented as an interval (l_i, r_i). Then:

- n_1 is a predecessor of $n_2 \Leftrightarrow l_1 < l_2$ and $r_1 > r_2$;
- n_2 is a predecessor of $n_1 \Leftrightarrow l_2 < l_1$ and $r_2 > r_1$;
- n_1 and n_2 are unrelated $\Leftrightarrow (l_1 > l_2 \wedge r_1 > r_2)$ or $(l_1 < l_2 \wedge r_1 < r_2)$.

All successors of a node can be determined by finding all the intervals that include the interval of the node. Similarly, all predecessors (e.g., the lineage) can be determined by finding all the intervals that enclose the interval of this node. We store this information in a relation of the form TC(node_id, left, right). The query for determining the lineage of a node with node_id nid then is:

```
SELECT tc2.node_id
  FROM TC AS tc1, TC AS tc2
 WHERE tc1.node_id = nid AND
       tc2.left < tc1.left AND
       tc1.right < tc2.right
```

Unfortunately, tree encoding cannot be used on arbitrary DAGs. Hence we cannot compare it directly with the other two techniques. We have nevertheless performed an experiment on randomly generated trees with between 5 and 100 nodes. The results of finding the lineage of a leaf in the tree are shown in Figure 13.3. The result, compared with the previous results, is that the running time is very stable independently of the size of the tree and the overhead is actually very low compared to the times for recursive queries or queries over all paths. Such is the behavior that we aim to achieve when encoding arbitrary DAGs.

13.2. Encoding DAGs With Intervals

13.2.1. Overview

Arbitrary DAGs cannot always be encoded using one-dimensional intervals. This can be easily illustrated with the example DAG depicted in Figure 13.4. The intervals representing nodes A, B, and C must have overlapping regions because they have common

13. Efficient Lineage Storage

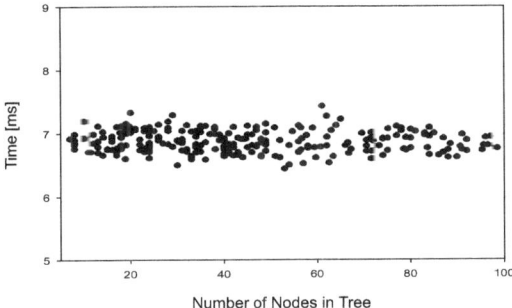

Figure 13.3.: Response time for queries for a tree stored with the directed tree encoding.

successors. No matter how the intervals are arranged, one of the intervals for D, E, or F will end up having a predecessor that does not exist in the real graph.

This can be formally proven, however, here we just outline the proof. For the intervals A, B, and C to overlap, but not enclose each other, there is one intersection between two of these intervals that will always be completely enclosed by the third interval. Hence, intervals in that intersection will be successors of the first two intervals but also of the third. There is no possibility to have successors of the two intervals that are not also successors of the third.

The graph of Figure 13.4 can be encoded by using two-dimensional intervals (rectangles in the plane) instead of one-dimensional intervals. However, if we use rectangles in the plane, there are instances where the same situation arises in two dimensions. Given any number of dimensions, one can always come up with a graph that needs more dimensions to be encoded. In what follows, we explore the problem more formally.

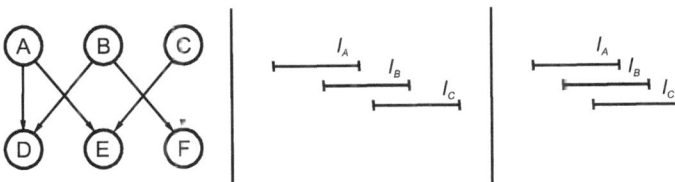

Figure 13.4.: The graph (left) cannot be encoded with intervals: with the only two interval assignments in which $I_A \& I_B$ and $I_B \& I_C$ can have common successors, $I_A \& I_C$ cannot have common successors (middle) and all common successors of $I_A \& I_C$ must also be successor of I_B (right).

13.2.2. Graph Encoding

The problem of encoding dependency graphs has been extensively studied in the literature.

The set of directed acyclic graphs that can be encoded with intervals is called the class of *interval containment graphs* [66]. More generally, the family of graphs that can be encoded with d-dimensional objects in Euclidean space is called *containment graphs*.

The number of dimensions needed to encode a graph can be determined from the structure of the graph. A directed acyclic graph $G = (V, E)$ represents a partially ordered set (*poset*) P of the nodes V of G: $P = (V, <)$. In the poset P, $i, j \in V$ are comparable ($i < j$) if $[i, j] \in E$ or $[j, i] \in E$. In other words, two nodes i and j are comparable if G contains a directed path from i to j or from j to i. Otherwise, if neither $[i, j] \notin E$ nor $[j, i] \notin E$, i.e., no path linking them exists in G, then i and j are incomparable. The dimension of a poset is defined as the minimum size k of the realizer of P, where the realizer is a collection of linear orders $L_1 = (V, <_1), ..., L_k = (V, <_k)$ such that $x < y$ if $x <_i y \ \forall i$, or $P = \bigcap_{i=1}^{k} L_i$ [33]. The number of dimensions necessary to encode the graph is a function of the dimension of the poset of the graph [42] as follows:

- if the dimension of the poset is at most 2, then the dimension d of the objects required to represent G is 1, meaning that G can be represented by intervals on the line (i.e., one-dimensional intervals) [34].

- if the dimension of the poset represented by G is at most $2d$, then the objects required to represent G are boxes in d-dimensional Euclidean space [42].

From here it follows that there is no encoding with a fixed number of dimensions that can perfectly encode arbitrary DAGs. For trees, the poset has dimension 2 [122]. This is why a tree can be encoded with intervals in one-dimensional space.

13.2.3. Related Complexity Results

Testing if the dimension of a poset is no bigger than 2 can be solved in polynomial time [123]. The problem of determining the dimension of a poset bigger than 2, however, is NP-complete [42].

Testing whether the dimension of the poset is 2 can be done by testing whether the incomparability graph $I_G = (V, E_{IG})$ of $G = (V, E)$ is transitively orientable [123]. The incomparability graph I_G can be derived from G by adding to E_{IG} an undirected edge if $x, y \in V$ are not comparable, i.e., if x, y do not have any predecessor/successor relationship. Testing whether a graph is transitively orientable can be done in polynomial time [95] or even in linear time [76].

Determining if a given graph is an interval containment graph, and can therefore be encoded with intervals on the line, can also be determined by finding forbidden subgraphs. If a graph contains any induced subgraph of a known set (defined in [105, 113]) then it is not an interval containment graph. The set of forbidden subgraphs is limited to a small number of graphs. One strategy for transforming an arbitrary graph into a graph with a poset of dimension 2 is to detect any forbidden subgraphs it might contain and transform the forbidden subgraphs into subgraphs of poset dimension 2 while maintaining the transitive closure. Unfortunately, detecting forbidden subgraphs is related to the problem of subgraph isomorphism which is NP-complete [114].

13.3. Transformation Algorithm

Our goal is to come up with a transformation algorithm that takes an arbitrary DAG as input and outputs an equivalent DAG (with the same transitive closure) that can be encoded with one-dimensional intervals. A brute force approach is to take the DAG and transform it into a tree by duplicating nodes. The result is an optimized version of the "all paths" approach (the optimization arises from not having to replicate common subpaths). Yet the behavior is similar to storing all the paths. We can also not just replace the forbidden subgraphs with tree structures because finding them is NP-complete.

What we can do, however, is to determine whether a subgraph has a poset of dimension 2 or higher. Thus, we can take the original DAG, find its incomparability graph, determine the independent subgraphs of the incomparability graph, and check for each one of those subgraphs whether they are transitively orientable (which can be done in polynomial time, see above). If they are, they can be encoded with intervals. If they are not, their corresponding subgraph in the DAG needs to be transformed. Note that this is not the same as finding induced forbidden subgraphs (which is NP-complete as indicated above).

Each of the identified problematic subgraphs of the DAG is transformed into a tree through node duplication. Optimizations are applied to minimize the space overhead generated by node duplication. The trees are then glued back into the original graph. Once the transformation is complete, we proceed with the interval encoding. We refer to this approach as interval encoding for DAGs or IDAG.

The approach is summarized in Algorithm 1. In what follows we describe in detail how the algorithm works by explaining each one of its functions computing the incomparability graph, finding independent subgraphs, testing for transitive orientability, transformation to a tree and optimizations. We also describe how the encoding works.

13. Efficient Lineage Storage

Algorithm 1 High-level view of the algorithm used to reduce the dimension of an arbitrary DAG.

Algorithm: Transformation Algorithm
Input: graph: input DAG

```
1 Graph icgraph = computeIncomparabilityGraph(graph)
2 foreach subgraph in independentSubgraphs(icgraph) do
3     if dimension(subgraph) > 2 then
4         optimize(subgraph)
5         transformToTree(subgraph)
6     end
7 end
```

13.3.1. computeIncomparabilityGraph($graph$)

The incomparability graph I_G has the same set of nodes as G, $V_{IG} = V$, but has a different set of edges E_{IG}: if two nodes $v_1, v_2 \in V$ have no transitive relation, then the undirected edge $(v_1, v_2) \in E_{IG}$. This means in particular that if v_1 and v_2 do not share a path, i.e., they are not part of the same total order over E (and hence not comparable in the partial order defined by G), then they are connected through an undirected edge in E_{IG}. Figure 13.5 (left) depicts a graph G and its corresponding incomparability graph I_G (middle).

To compute I_G efficiently, the algorithm uses a $|V|/2 \times |V|/2$ matrix C of booleans. $C[i,j]$ is true if there is a path between v_i and v_j $\forall i < j$. The matrix can be computed by traversing the graph in $O(|V|+|E|)$. Computing I_G from the matrix C only requires one pass over C and adding an undirected edge (v_i, v_j) to E_{IG} if $C[i,j]$ is false. This is done in $O(|V|^2)$.

13.3.2. independentSubgraphs($icgraph$)

The graph I_G may contain several subgraphs not connected to each other. Such an example is shown in Figure 13.5 (middle). These situations arise very often in real workflows. For instance when there are tasks that are in all possible paths (e.g., a start task like task A in Figure 13.5). The same situation arises at synchronization points for parallel threads (e.g., task G in Figure 13.5).

How these independent subgraphs arise can be illustrated using the example in Figure 13.5.

Assume there is a node s contained on all execution paths such that each other node $v \in V$ on each execution path, and total order is either $s < v$ or $v < s$. Consider two sets A and B. B contains all nodes $v \in V$ which satisfy $s < v$ in all total orders over G. A contains all nodes $v \in V$ which satisfy $v < s$ in all total orders over G. Note that $A \cap B = \emptyset$, as all nodes $v \in V$ are either before or after s on all execution paths. different total order. This implies that no total order is defined over these two vertices and hence $(a, v) \notin E$, breaking the assumption made before.) All nodes $v \in A$ are on

13. Efficient Lineage Storage

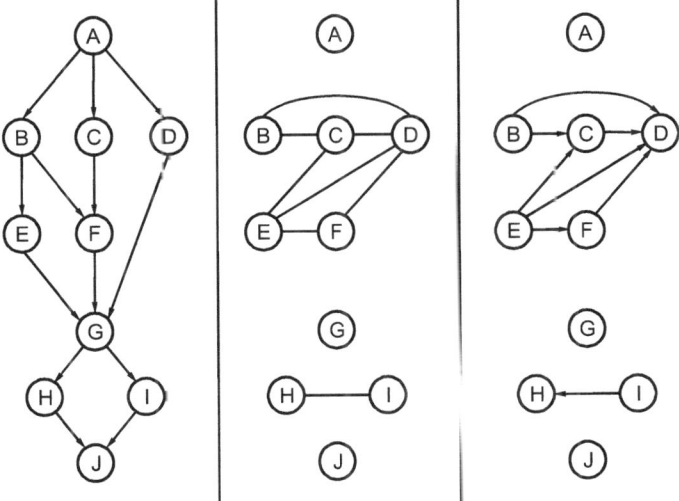

Figure 13.5.: The incomparability graph (middle) for a graph (left) and a possible transitive orientation of the incomparability graph (right).

a path through s. Thus in I_G there will not be any edge between any of the nodes in A and s as they are comparable in G. The same applies to B and s. Because every node in A reaches s and s reaches all the nodes in B, there will be no edges between nodes in A and nodes in B. Hence A, B and s result in independent subgraphs of the incomparability graph. This is the situation induced by node G in Figure 13.5.

Finding such subgraphs in I_G is important as they can be treated independently in determining their dimension and also in the reduction of their dimension as will be shown later. The independent subgraphs of I_G are identified by traversing I_G starting at each source (node with in-degree 0) and visiting all nodes which are connected to the source. This is done by traversing the graph in $O(|V| + |E|)$.

13.3.3. dimension(*cluster*)

Each independent subgraph of the incomparability graph I_G is tested separately. If the dimension of the partially ordered set represented by G is no higher than 2, then the incomparability graph I_G is transitively orientable. I_G is transitively orientable if for each edge in E_{IG}, a direction can be assigned such that all directions of the edges satisfy transitivity, i.e., if the directed edges (u, v) and $(v, w) \in \vec{E}_{IG}$ then there must also be a directed edge (u, w) in $\vec{E}_{IG}$.

13. Efficient Lineage Storage

Clearly, if I_G contains several independent subgraphs, the dimension of each of these subgraphs can be tested separately: as no undirected edge connects any two nodes of two independent subgraphs, each of the subgraphs must be transitively orientable for the entire graph to be transitively orientable. If one subgraph is not transitively orientable, only the dimension of this subgraph needs to be reduced. Then the subgraph becomes transitively orientable and, if this is the case for all subgraphs, the whole graph becomes transitively orientable as well.

Algorithm 2 Transitively orient an undirected graph.

Algorithm: Orient Transitively
Input: undirected subgraph of $G_{SIG} = (V_{SIG}, E_{SIG})$
Output: $\vec{E_{IG}}$: set of directed edges

1 $\vec{E_{IG}} \leftarrow \emptyset$
2 choose arbitrary $edge \in E_{SIG}$, remove $edge$ from E_{SIG}
3 direct $edge$ arbitrarily: (u,v), add $edge$ to $\vec{E_{SIG}}$
4 **repeat**
5   test if any edge incident to $edge$ in E_{SIG} with (v,w), assign to I_v
6   test if any edge incident to $edge$ in E_{SIG} with (t,u), assign to I_u
7   **if** $I_v = I_u = \emptyset \land E_{SIG} \neq \emptyset$ **then**
8   choose arbitrary $edge \in E_{SIG}$
9   remove $edge$ from E_{SIG}
10   **end**
11   **foreach** $incident \in I_v$ **do**
12   **if** $(u,w) \notin E_{SIG}$ **then**
13   direct $incident$ (w,v), add to $\vec{E_{SIG}}$
14   remove $incident$ from E_{SIG}
15   **end**
16   **end**
17   **foreach** $incident \in I_u$ **do**
18   **if** $(t,v) \notin E_{SIG}$ **then**
19   direct $incident$ (u,t), add to $\vec{E_{SIG}}$
20   remove $incident$ from E_{SIG}
21   **end**
22   **end**
23 **until** $E_{SIG} = \emptyset$;

We use a polynomial time algorithm to test if a subgraph is transitively orientable [95]. Given an undirected subgraph $G_{SIG} = (V_{SIG}, E_{SIG})$ of I_G, the algorithm initially picks a random undirected edge $e \in E_{SIG}$, removes e from E_{SIG}, directs it arbitrarily and adds the resulting $\vec{e}$ to a set of directed edges called $\vec{E_{SIG}}$. It then tries to direct as many edges as possible by taking an edge $\vec{e}$ out of $\vec{E_{SIG}}$ and directing all undirected edges $e \in E_{SIG}$ incident to the source or destination of $\vec{e}$. The incident edges are directed such that giving each incident edge a direction will not violate the transitivity property. This

13. Efficient Lineage Storage

means for a directed edge $\vec{e} = (u,v)$, that if an edge f incident to v is directed such that $\vec{f} = (v,w)$ then there must also exist an edge g which can be directed $\vec{g} = (u,w)$ in order to maintain the transitivity property. Otherwise, f must be directed such that $\vec{f} = (w,v)$.

More formally, the edges incident to a directed edge $\vec{e} = (u,v)$ are directed according to the following rule: an undirected edge $d = (t,u)$ incident to the source u of $\vec{e}$, is directed such that $\vec{d} = (u,t)$ and added to $\vec{E_{SIG}}$, if $(t,v) \notin E_{SIG}$. This leaves the two directed edges $\vec{d} = (u,t)$ and $\vec{e} = (u,v)$. If the edges were directed $\vec{d} = (t,u)$ and $\vec{e} = (u,v)$ or $\vec{d} = (u,t)$ and $\vec{e} = (v,u)$ then E_{SIG} would be required to contain an edge $f = (t,v)$ (which would be required to be directed accordingly in order to maintain transitivity). The edges incident to the destination of $\vec{e}$ are directed using the same rule. The newly directed edges are removed from E_{SIG} and added to $\vec{E_{SIG}}$.

The algorithm directs edges according to this rule as long as there are undirected edges in E_{SIG} and as long as there are directed edges in $\vec{E_{SIG}}$ with undirected edges incident to either their source or destination. Once no such edges are left in E_{SIG}, a random edge is chosen from E_{SIG} and is directed arbitrarily. The algorithm then again continues to direct the edges using the same rule.

The procedure is sketched in Algorithm 2. The algorithm finishes once all edges are directed. What follows is a test of the transitivity of the graph defined by $(V, \vec{E_{SIG}})$. For this, all edges $\vec{e} = (u,v) \in \vec{E_{SIG}}$ are tested iteratively. Particularly, given $\vec{e}$, if there exists a $\vec{f} = (v,w)$, then $\vec{E_{SIG}}$ must also contain a directed edge (u,w). If this is not the case for all $\vec{e} \in \vec{E_{SIG}}$ then $(V, \vec{E_{SIG}})$ is not transitively orientable.

13.3.4. optimize(*cluster*)

It is possible that within an independent subgraph of the incomparability graph that is not transitively orientable, there are parts that can be encoded. Consider, as an example, the shaded subgraph of the graph in Figure 13.6 (left). Such a subgraph is a common pattern in workflows that execute sets of parallel tasks [117]. The graph as a whole cannot be encoded, but the shaded subgraph can as it is of dimension 2. There are many workflow patterns that share this property of being of dimension 2 and which therefore do not need to be transformed into a tree (e.g., a sequential chain of tasks). However they might be embedded into larger graphs that cannot be encoded. An obvious optimization is to detect these patterns before proceeding with the transformation of the whole graph into a tree.

Instead of trying to detect patterns, the algorithm identifies subgraphs and tests for their dimension. If the dimension is no higher than 2, then the subgraph does not need to be transformed. Then, in practice, the subgraphs which do not need to be transformed are removed from the graph and replaced with a placeholder node. The graph is then converted and, after the transformation, the removed subgraphs are put back in the graph.

The subgraphs to be identified by the algorithm have one common property: they all contain two designated nodes of which a first node i is the only node in the subgraph which is the destination of edges outside the subgraph and the second node o is the only node in the subgraph which is the source of edges leading outside the subgraph. The subgraph between i and o, S_G is then tested for its dimension. If it is of dimension higher than 2, then the subgraphs in S_G are again tested.

Finding the subgraphs with the property described above is done by testing all possible pairs of nodes and checking to see if they are on the same set of paths in $O(|V|^2)$. This check can be done using the matrix C introduced in Section 13.3.1.

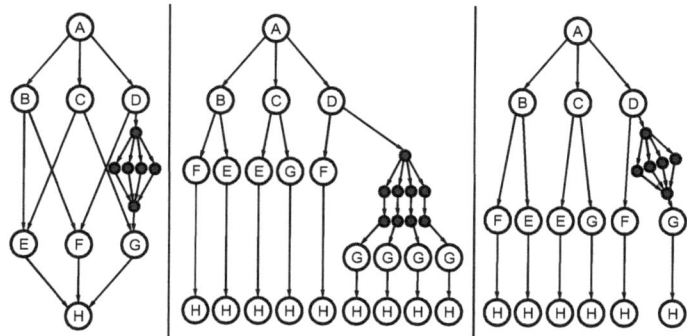

Figure 13.6.: Illustration of the transformation optimization. The initial graph (left), the corresponding transformed tree (middle) and the optimized transformed tree (right).

13.3.5. transformToTree(*cluster*)

If an incomparability subgraph is not transitively orientable, then the corresponding dependency subgraph needs to be transformed into a tree while maintaining the transitive closure of the dependency subgraph. Algorithm 3 traverses the subgraph and in case a node with an in-degree in greater than 1 is visited, then this node will be copied $in-1$ times. For each of the copied nodes, also the outgoing edges of the node are also copied. The in incoming edges of v will be reconnected to the $in-1$ copies and to the node. Reconnecting the incoming edges to the copies ensures that each of the resulting nodes has an in-degree of at most 1, thus ensuring that the resulting graph is indeed a tree. Also, connecting each incoming edge of the node to a copy ensures that the transitive closure is preserved. Figure 13.7 illustrates how the algorithm works. The algorithm is equivalent to a graph traversal, hence its complexity is $O(|V|+|E|)$.

The tree is inserted into the original graph by first removing all the nodes and edges of the problematic subgraph and then gluing the tree in its place.

13. Efficient Lineage Storage

Algorithm 3 Algorithm used to transform an arbitrary DAG into a tree while maintaining the transitive closure.

Algorithm: Tree Transformation
Input: graph: directed subgraph of $G_S = (V_{SG}, E_{SG})$

1 **foreach** $node \in V_{SG}$ **do**
2   **if** *in-degree of node > 1* **then**
3   **foreach** *edge of all incoming edges - 1 of node* **do**
4   copy node
5   set copy as destination of edge
6   **foreach** *edge of all outgoing edges of node* **do**
7   copy edge
8   set copy as source of edge
9   **end**
10   **end**
11   **end**
12 **end**

13.3.6. Interval Assignment

Subsequent to the graph transformation, each node in the graph needs to be assigned an interval on the line. The graph, which is going to be encoded, is the result of the transformation algorithm discussed before and hence we can assume that it is encodable with intervals, i.e. it represents a poset of dimension 2.

The interval assignment of such a graph can be determined by using two linear extensions realizing the poset defined by G. In order to compute two linear extensions, the transitive orientation of the incomparability graph I_G of graph G is required. Since G has been modified, the transitive orientation has to be computed again by using the procedures described in Sections 13.3.1, 13.3.2 and 13.3.3.

Two linear extensions can then be computed by traversing the graph from sources to sinks, visiting each node only once its predecessors have been visited. If several nodes are ready to be visited, they are by definition incomparable and are visited in the order of the transitive orientation to obtain the first linear extension. For the second extension, the incomparable nodes are visited in the reverse order of the transitive orientation. The intuition behind this is that in one linear order the two incomparable nodes x, y must occur $x < y$ while in the other order they must occur $y < x$. The case in which several nodes are ready to be visited occurs if they have no predecessor/successor relationship. Hence they are incomparable and therefore their order is defined in the transitive orientation of the incomparability graph.

Assume two linear orders $L, \overline{L}$ realizing the partial order P on the set of vertices V of graph G (the dimension of the poset therefore is 2). L defines an order over V whereas $\overline{L}$ defines an order over a copy of V called $\overline{V}$ in which the elements are renamed, e.g., x becomes $\overline{x}$. The two linear orders are then appended such that $L = L_2 + L_1^{-1}$, where

13. Efficient Lineage Storage

L_1^{-1} is simply the inverse of L_1 such that if $x, y \in V$ with $x < y \in L_1$, then $y < x \in L_1^{-1}$. L then has the following properties:

- if two vertices $x, y \in V$ are comparable and if $x < y$ (in L_2) then $\bar{y} < \bar{x}$ (in L_1^{-1}) and vice versa. Hence in this case in L: $x < y < \bar{y} < \bar{x}$.

- if two vertices $x, y \in V$ are not comparable, then $x < y$ in L_2 and $\bar{x} < \bar{y}$ in L_1^{-1} (because it is $\bar{y} < \bar{x}$ in L_1) and in this case in L: $x < y < \bar{x} < \bar{y}$.

L will then allow us to easily label all the nodes in the graph. If two nodes x, y have a predecessor/successor relationship, they are comparable and in case they have no such relationship they are not comparable. Assume each element in L is labeled increasing from left to right, each node x will be assigned the interval $I_x = [x, \bar{x}]$. Then if two elements x, y are comparable, they have a predecessor/successor relationship and then, as discussed previously, L: $x < y < \bar{y} < \bar{x}$. From the assignment of intervals follows that I_x will enclose I_y. If x, y are not comparable, they have no predecessor/successor relationship and, L: $x < y < \bar{x} < \bar{y}$. I_x and I_y will therefore overlap. The semantic of I_x enclosing I_y depends on the relation $<$ used in the poset. If $x < y$ implies x is a predecessor of y, then I_x will enclose I_y and vice versa.

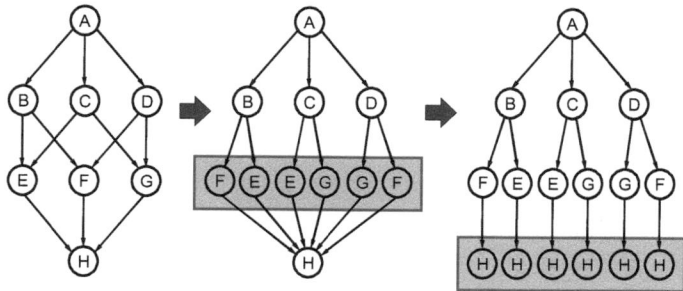

Figure 13.7.: Illustration of the transformation of a graph into a tree.

The complexity of computing the transitively oriented incomparability graph has been derived in Sections 13.3.1, 13.3.2 and 13.3.3. After transitively orienting G, all that is left to be done in order to assign an interval for each node, is to traverse the graph. The complexity of this step is $O(|V| + |E|)$.

13.4. Evaluation

13.4.1. Evaluation Setup

To demonstrate the feasibility and competitive advantage of our approach, we have carried out experiments for two classes of graphs, the first being random DAGs and the second being a set of representative and interesting use cases of scientific workflows.

For the evaluation of our approach we have performed experiments to measure the overhead of the graph transformation and interval assignment. Additionally, we have also measured the response time for a lineage query (the lineage of a randomly selected leaf node) as well as the number of tuples to be stored for a graph. We compare the numbers obtained with the two other approaches, querying over all paths and recursive queries.

The setup used was the same throughout all experiments: two nodes in a cluster of Linux machines (dual Opteron 2.4 GHz machines with 2 GB memory) connected with a 1Gb/s local area network were used. One node hosted a Postgres 8.2.1 database where the graph information was stored while the other node hosted the client. The client performed the calculations, the transformation of the graph as well as the interval assignment, and issued all queries.

Random DAGs are not very realistic representations of scientific workflows. Many optimizations we have proposed do not apply, even though they are very common in real workflows. Yet random graphs can be seen as a worst case scenario for comparison purposes.

13.4.2. Evaluation on Random DAGs

In a first set of experiments we generated random DAGs and, if necessary, applied the transformation to them. The resulting graph was assigned intervals for each node and was stored in the database. Each random DAG was assigned a random number of nodes between 5 and 100 and each node was assigned between 1 and 4 outgoing edges to other randomly chosen nodes. The edges were assigned such that the addition of an outgoing edge did not lead to a cycle in the graph.

Preprocessing

In a first experiment we measured the overhead of transforming the graph. For the all paths approach, this involves computing all paths in the graph, whereas, in the case of the interval encoding, this includes the graph transformation and the interval assignment. The recursive queries approach does not require any preprocessing: the relationships or edges are directly stored in the database. Thus, we exclude it from this comparison.

The time required to preprocess the graph in both approaches does not directly depend on the number of nodes in the graph but rather on the structure of the graph. It can, however, generally be assumed that the more nodes a graph has, the more complex

13. Efficient Lineage Storage

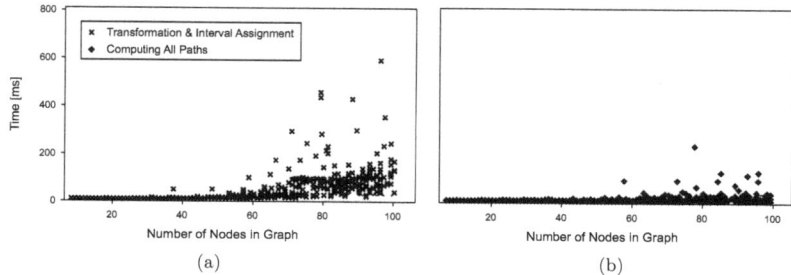

Figure 13.8.: Time required to preprocess a random DAG.

its structure is going to be (this is particularly true for random DAGs). Figure 13.8 shows that the time required for the preprocessing is generally higher the more nodes a graph has. In general, the storing all paths approach performs better than the interval encoding approach. This is not surprising, given that the interval encoding approach also needs to compute all paths in the graph. Note, however, that the preprocessing is done offline and only once, hence the overhead is acceptable.

Querying

Figure 13.9 shows a comparison of the three approaches regarding response time. For each DAG, a query asking for all predecessors of a leaf (e.g., the lineage of the node) was issued.

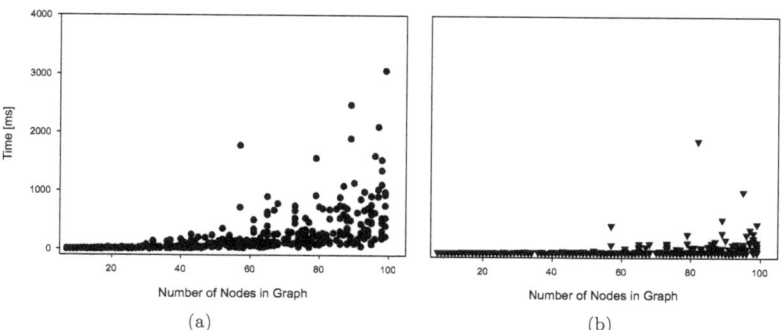

Figure 13.9.: Response time over random DAGs for the recursive (a) and all paths approach (b).

13. Efficient Lineage Storage

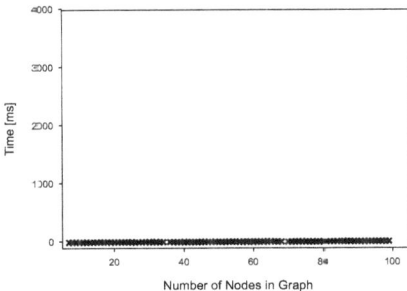

Figure 13.10.: Response time over random DAGs for the interval encoding approach

Figure 13.9 (a) clearly indicates that the recursive approach does not scale very well with graphs having an increasing number of nodes. While in some cases the response time is in line with the other two approaches, there are many cases where the running time is much higher. Figure 13.9 (b) & Figure 13.10 illustrate the difference between our approach and storing all paths. In the majority of cases, the interval encoding approach clearly outperforms the storing all paths approach.

Storage Size

It is also important to measure the storage space required by each approach. In this experiment we have therefore compared how many tuples are required to store the transitive closure information of the DAGs.

The number of tuples required to store the transitive closure in case of the recursive approach is equal to the number of edges in the graph. Clearly, no other approach will require less tuples. In Figure 13.11 we compare the amount of storage required by all paths and that required by interval encoding.

As was to be expected, storing all paths in the graph requires the largest number of tuples. The number of tuples required roughly scales linear with the number of paths in the graph. Our approach with the optimized transformation into an encodable graph requires significantly less tuples to store the transitive closure.

13.4.3. Evaluation on Scientific Workflows

In the next series of experiments we compare the different approaches using a set of real scientific workflows: fMRI, Montage and EMAN (Figure 13.12). These three workflows have interesting structures that make them particularly suitable for our experiments. The fMRI workflow serves as an example of a small static acyclic workflow which makes use of parallelism to speed up the computation. The EMAN workflow iterates over a loop to improve the overall quality of the result. By doing so, it leads to dependency

13. Efficient Lineage Storage

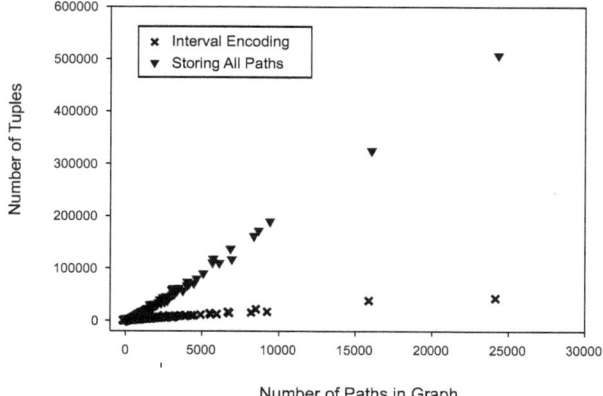

Figure 13.11.: Storage space requirements.

graphs of very large depth. The Montage workflow on the other hand does not have the depth of the EMAN workflow, but it is massively parallel.

Functional Magnetic Resonance Imaging (fMRI)

The functional magnetic resonance imaging workflow (fMRI) [54] is used to process raw data of brain scans. It takes in a first step the raw data, aligns it to a reference brain image by reslicing it, averages over several scans executed with different wavelengths, and finally slices along the x, y and z dimensions. The structure is reasonably simple, with two phases of parallel program executions, the first phase ending at the averaging over all scans (where all execution paths meet) and the second starting thereafter.

Although being the smallest workflow we use in the experiments, it is not a simple workflow in terms of structure as it has to be transformed (the first phase of the parallel program executions). Thus, from the original size of 45 nodes, it is transformed into a graph of 107 nodes. The increase, however, is still modest in comparison, as the approach storing all paths would require 2496 tuples.

Figure 13.13 compares the response time (left) for a lineage query over the fMRI workflow encoded using the three approaches. The interval encoding approach clearly outperforms the others, especially the recursive approach. As it is shown in Figure 13.13 (right), the storing all paths approach performs reasonably well regarding response time, but requires twice the number of tuples. The preprocessing takes 46.27ms for interval encoding, 9.7ms for the storing all paths approach and no time for the recursive approach.

13. Efficient Lineage Storage

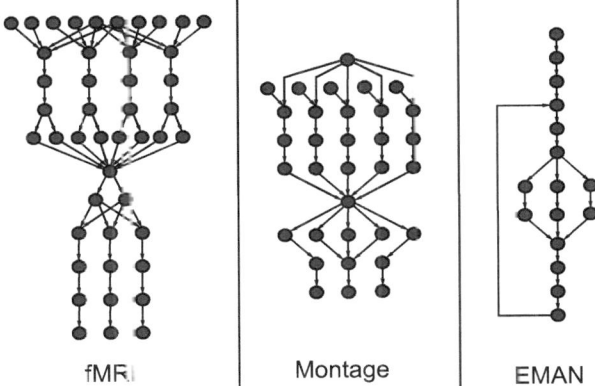

Figure 13.12.: Dependency graphs for three scientific workflows: fMRI, Montage and EMAN (left to right).

Astronomical Image Mosaic (Montage)

The Montage workflow [10] was developed as part of the National Virtual Observatory (NVO), aiming at processing raw instrument data or images from telescopes and assembling them into a mosaic out of many (possibly hundreds) pieces of data. The workflow runs through several stages, starting by transferring the input files in parallel, reprojecting and fitting them into a common plane. The execution paths of the workflow then converge in the background modeling node, subsequently go through the background correction and finally through the assembly of the image stages in parallel. The degree of parallelism of the phases before and after the background modeling depends on the number of input files to be processed. Smaller instances of the workflow typically assemble more than 40 input files, resulting in 40 parallel execution threads leading to a dependency graph of more than 1000 nodes.

Figure 13.14 (top) shows the space required by the different approaches to store the transitive closure of the montage workflow depending on the number of input files. Since this workflow does not need transformation, both the recursive approach and the interval encoding do not require much space. The all paths approach requires considerably more space and the space needed grows significantly with the number of input files, making it unsuitable for this type of workflow.

Figure 13.14 (bottom) shows the response time as a function of the number of input files processed. While the recursive approach grows almost exponentially, the other two approaches grow linearly, interval encoding being clearly better.

13. Efficient Lineage Storage

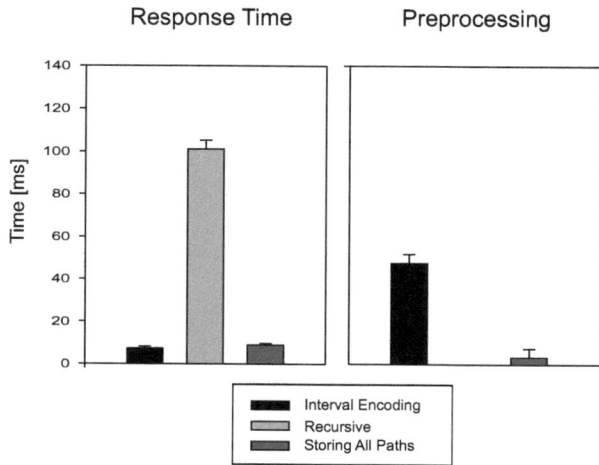

Figure 13.13.: Comparison of the response time for queries and time for the calculation for fMRI.

Electron Micrograph Analysis (EMAN)

The EMAN workflow [72, 104] processes thousands of micrographs from electron microscopes, iteratively trying to determine a macromolecular structure. The goal of the computation is to fit individual micrographs of particles, like viruses or proteins (ion channels) to a hypothetical 3D structure. More precisely, images of nanoscale molecules embedded in ice are collected and are analyzed with an electron microscope. A 3D model is then built using the EMAN workflow. The workflow runs through several potentially parallel stages and, depending on the resolution of the required 3D model, iterates through several refinement loops.

The structure of the workflow does not require any transformation. Thus, in case of one iteration, the space required to store the transitive closure is fairly small. Figure 13.15 (top) compares the space required to store the transitive closure of the three approaches depending on the number of iterations of the refinement loop. As before, recursive queries and interval encoding require constant space, while the space required by the storing all paths approach grows exponentially.

Figure 13.15 (bottom) shows the response time for queries using the different approaches with respect to the number of iterations over the refinement loops.

Figure 13.15 clearly demonstrate the benefits of our approach. The recursive approach does not require much space but its performance is not acceptable as the complexity of the workflow increases. Storing all paths has acceptable performance, but requires exponential growth in space as the complexity of the workflow grows. Interval encoding

13. Efficient Lineage Storage

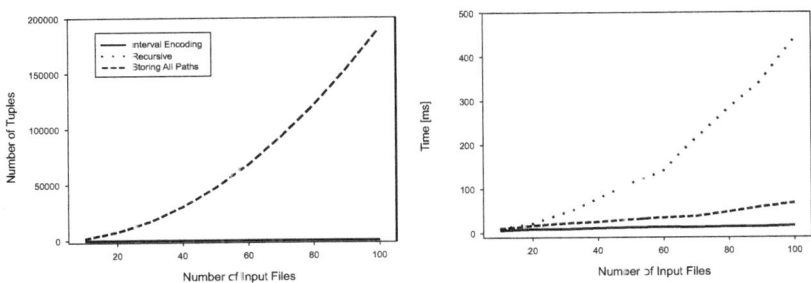

Figure 13.14.: Space requirements for the Montage workflow (top) and response time (bottom).

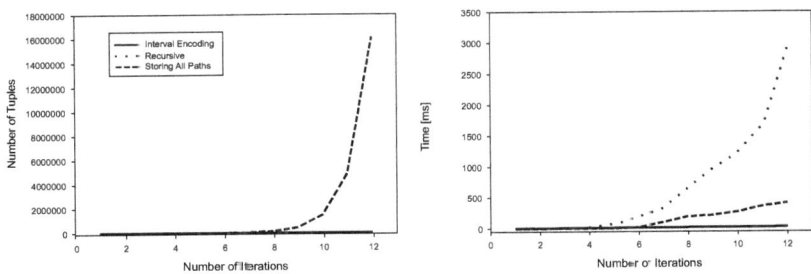

Figure 13.15.: Space requirements for the EMAN workflow (top) and response time (bottom).

requires very little space for storage and has the best performance, independently of the number of iterations and, hence, independently of the size and complexity of the graph.

14. Sisyphus Use Case

In this chapter we discuss using the IDAG approach to encode the fine-grained lineage information in Sisyphus. To do so, we introduce the concrete use case in Section 14.1. We also describe the pipeline used to process raw experiment results, the trans-proteomic pipeline (TPP). Section 14.2 describes how the relevant lineage information of the TPP is recorded and made available for querying to the user. The structure of the lineage information is also discussed, motivating the need for flexible encoding mechanisms. We thoroughly discuss different alternatives of encoding the data in Section 14.3. In Section 14.4, we present measurements regarding the performance for both storing and querying the lineage information. We conclude this chapter Section 14.5 discuses the implementation of the appropriate encoding in the Sisyphus system.

14.1. Project Background

Analyzing huge amounts of experiments in systems biology disciplines like cell surface proteomics has only been made possible through the application of mass spectrometry and due to recent advances in the computational tools used to process raw mass spectrometry data. These computational tools allow scientists to visualize and interpret the experiment data but also make tracking and storing lineage information of paramount importance. In the following, we give an overview of the biological background as well as the processing pipeline used throughout the paper.

14.1.1. Cell Surface Proteomics

Proteomics is the large scale study of the function and structure of proteins. As opposed to the genome of an organism, the proteome, the collection of all its proteins, changes over time. The exact proteome of a cell depends on many factors, but most importantly on the interactions with other cells. Of particular interest are proteins on the cell surface. Being able to determine the proteome of cell surfaces will help to understand cell-cell interactions and thereby will give a much better understanding of the organism. Novel methods have been developed to isolate the proteins on the cell surface, allowing for the first time to specifically study and analyze the cell surface proteome.

However, many samples of the cell surface need to be analyzed in order to gain an understanding of the interactions between cells. The limited throughput of traditional approaches for analyzing samples regarding quality and quantity of the proteins, like protein sequencing or 2D gel-based approaches, has lead to the broad adoption of shotgun proteomics [82]. In shotgun proteomics, the mass distribution of peptides in a sample is determined by using mass spectrometers.

Tandem mass spectrometry is used to analyze a sample and to determine quality and quantity of the proteins contained in it. The basic idea of using mass spectrometry is to vaporize the sample and then to ionize it. After acceleration though a magnetic field, the beam of elements is directed into another magnetic field. The single particles are redirected based on their mass, yielding the mass distribution of the entire sample. Using the mass distribution, the initial particles of the sample can be inferred.

This process is however not without difficulty: charging proteins breaks them up into peptides, the next smaller unit. To work around the problem, enzymes are used to control the splitting. What is determined with mass spectrometry is thus no longer the mass spectra of the proteins, but the mass distribution of each of the peptides contained in the sample. Thus an additional step is needed to infer the proteins in the sample from the mass spectra. For this, a computational pipeline, the trans-proteomic pipeline (TPP) is used.

14.1.2. Trans-Proteomic Pipeline (TPP)

The trans-proteomic pipeline is a collection of loosely coupled software tools. The pipeline is released as a whole, but single tools can be replaced if newer versions become available.

Software Tools

In the first step of the pipeline, the results of the mass spectrometry, which are in an equipment and vendor specific format, are transformed into a standardized common file format. This file is then used to assign candidate peptides to each mass spectrum based on a database containing all peptides and proteins known to date.

Given the amino acid sequence of a peptide from the database, a hypothetical mass spectra is computed. The hypothetical spectra are then matched with the actual ones from the experiment. Several software packages [124, 94, 26], each implementing a different underlying model, can be used to match the spectra to the peptide's acid sequence. The process of matching the spectra to a peptide is ambiguous, and depends on the model used. Each assignment is thus given a confidence value (the probability that the match is indeed correct).

In a next step, the peptides are matched to proteins. This is a many-to-some relationship in that several peptides indicate the occurrence of a protein. This process is also ambiguous: one peptide may indicate several proteins. The result of this step is thus a list of proteins, each again with a probability assigned indicating the chances that it is actually present in the sample. In the next steps, applications are used to validate first the assignment of spectra to peptides and, in a next step, to assign proteins to peptides (using PeptideProphet[1] and ProteinProphet[2] respectively). Finally, proteins

---
[1] http://peptideprophet.sourceforge.net/
[2] http://proteinprophet.sourceforge.net/

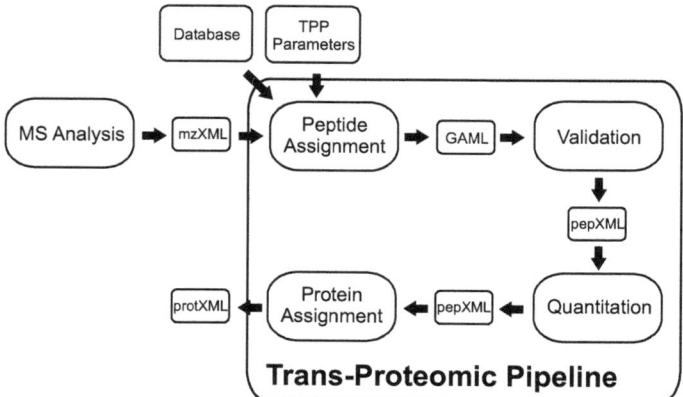

Figure 14.1.: The Trans-Proteomic Pipeline

and peptides are quantified using XPressRatio[3] and Libra[4]. The TPP is depicted in Figure 14.1.

The tools of the pipeline can be replaced with other versions or other tools. Tools are often appended to the processing pipeline for further analysis or visualization.

Data in the TPP

The TPP processes data in heterogeneous formats, all of them structured (XML) and well defined by schemas. It takes several files as input, among which is a file containing parameters for the TPP, the file to which the output will be written, the spectra over which it will be searched as well as the taxonomy file which contains references to the reference databases.

The files passed between the software tools are in different XML formats. The hierarchical structure of them models biological correlations. As an example, the output from the peptide validation is in the pepXML format. Such a file contains an array of spectrum queries (spectras), each containing the peptides or search hits which may match the spectrum. Each such search hit is assigned a number reflecting the probability of the match. The structure of a pepXML file is illustrated in Figure 14.2. The structure of a protXML file is similar: it contains an array of protein groups. Each protein group contains proteins which in turn contain the peptides out of which it is inferred.

---

[3] http://tools.proteomecenter.org/wiki/index.php?title=Software:XPRESS
[4] http://tools.proteomecenter.org/wiki/index.php?title=Software:Libra

14. Sisyphus Use Case

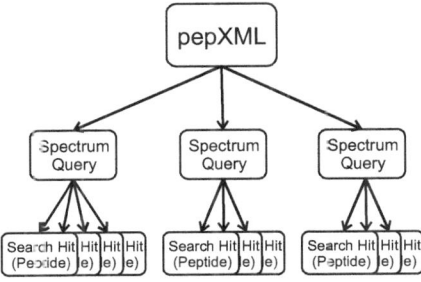

Figure 14.2.: Structure of a pepXML file

14.2. Lineage in the TPP

The trans-proteomic pipeline allows to track lineage on different levels of granularity. Coarse-grained lineage can be captured by instrumenting the TPP. Fine-grained lineage has to be extracted from the files passed in the TPP.

14.2.1. Coarse-grained Lineage

Coarse-grained or file-based lineage of the TPP can be recorded by instrumenting the workflow execution engine. With such instrumentation, one is able to exactly record what program execution has been using what file, what program execution has produced which file, etc. Most of the work based on workflow based data lineage addresses this type of lineage[79, 18, 14, 103].

14.2.2. Fine-grained Lineage

Relevant lineage information however allows to answer more detailed questions: 'What did have an influence on a specific inferred protein (or set of proteins)?', including all peptides, spectra, assignments and of course also the programs involved. This can be found by determining the items of interest at the right level of granularity (peptides, spectra or assignments), exploiting the structure of the data, and by connecting them with each another using the IDs uniquely identifying each item.

As an example, we will use the last part of the TPP to illustrate the pepXML file used by the ProteinProphet tool and the protXML file produced. Both, peptides and proteins in both files have a unique ID assigned. In case of the peptide, this is the amino acid sequence and in case of the protein an abstract ID. With these IDs it is possible to connect proteins to peptides as is depicted in Figure 14.3.

As mentioned earlier, the mapping of many items is ambiguous. This is also the case for the mapping of peptides to proteins shown in Figure 14.3. One protein has at least

14. Sisyphus Use Case

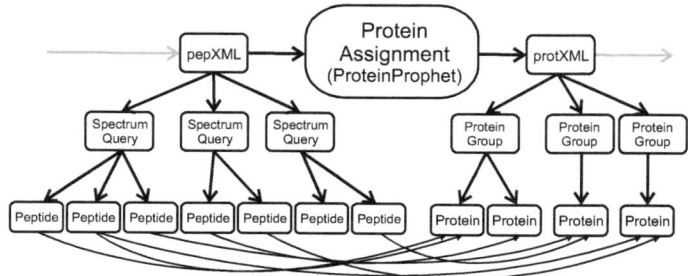

Figure 14.3.: Connecting the elements of interest in the pepXML and protXML in the last step of the TPP

one but usually several peptides it consists of. Also, a single peptide may contribute to several proteins suspected to be in the sample. The relationships between peptides and proteins therefore is many-to-many and consequently, the resulting structure cannot be represented by a tree.

Connecting input parameters, database entries, spectras, peptides and proteins, the fine-grained lineage information can be captured by a directed acyclic graph. Figure 14.4 illustrates a simplified DAG for just two protein inferences. One experiment processed by the TPP contains several hundred to thousands protein inferences, leading to a DAG with several thousand nodes. Note that such a graph does not contain independent subgraphs for each protein inference but is instead connected.

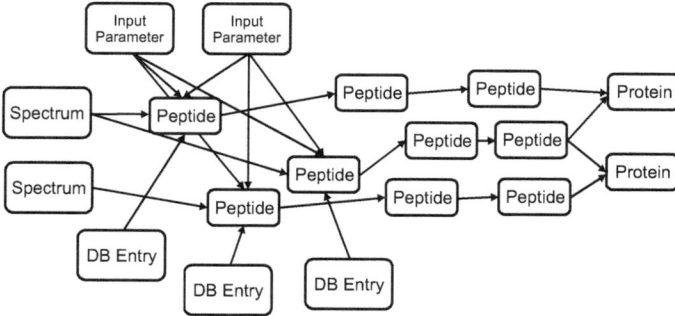

Figure 14.4.: DAG structure of the fine-grained lineage

108

14.2.3. Connecting Fine- & Coarse-Grained Lineage

The coarse-grained lineage information (e.g., what pepXML file has been used by the ProteinProphet execution) can be linked to the fine-grained information (e.g., what protein has been inferred by what peptide). This is necessary in order to be able to answer questions 'What protXML belongs this protein to?' or 'What version of ProteinProphet has been inferring this protein?'. It is therefore not enough to store the dependency (i.e, what has been causing what) but also the hierarchy (i.e., what is part of what). In contrast to the dependency relationships, the hierarchy relationship can be stored as a tree (as they are captured in the XML documents). Figure 14.3 illustrates this by associating peptides with spectrum queries which in turn are associated with a specific pepXML file. This can be done for all file involved in the execution of the TPP.

When storing all this lineage information, there are thus three different types of information to deal with: *attributes* (protein groups, files, program executions, etc.), *hierarchy relationships*, and *dependency relationships*.

The example questions listed below use such information as follows:

Question 1: an example question a biologist may ask 'What file contained the mass spectra from which a specific protein was inferred from?'. Such a question would first identify one or several proteins given some attribute, then use a dependency query to find out what mass spectra were used to infer it and finally use a hierarchical query to identify the file these mass spectra are contained in. Answering a question like this is important as it allows the biologists to identify what file containing raw experiment data needs to be processed again in case of errors.

Question 2: similarly, an equally important question is 'What programs were involved in inferring a specific protein?'. Since there is no direct dependency relation between proteins and the programs used to infer them, a hierarchical query first has to ask for the result file where the protein is found and then ask what programs produced such a file using a dependency query.

Question 3: a different question may be 'What other proteins were inferred from the same raw input data file along with a suspicious and possibly wrong protein and may therefore also be wrong?' This questions extends example question 1 by subsequently querying what files were derived from this raw input file and what proteins are contained in it.

This is of course not an exhaustive list of possible questions but illustrates the variety, complexity and types of questions and how they can be answered using dependency and hierarchy queries.

14.2.4. Tracking and Storing the Lineage

The tools which are part of the TPP are wrapped in scripts which are orchestrated with a workflow. The scripts wrapping the tools take the same arguments as the actual tool and are used to extract the parameters, the input and output files as well as attributes of the tool. These scripts register program executions, parameters, data and the relationships between programs and data.

Inferring Hierarchy

Once a script is executed it will store the relevant attributes of the files used and produced. In addition to that, it can also store the hierarchical relationships between data items. For this, the script will look at the structured contents of the file and will use handlers for each type of data item contained. In case of pepXML, for instance, the script parses the pepXML file and will for each spectrum query in it call a handler to store it and associate it with the file. Following this, the search hits (peptides) will be parsed and again, for each search hit, a handler will be called for storing it in the DB and for associating it with the spectrum query. Scripts and handlers for all files and data items processed by the TPP have been implemented.

Inferring Dependency

Inferring the causality happens on two different levels. The relationships of the coarse-grained lineage information are captured by the workflow execution engine and the scripts wrapping of the tools. These scripts register program executions and the files used and generated. By identifying what files are equal, the scripts can connect producer and consumer of data and establish a dependency connection. For this, scripts need to know what files are equal. The script having a file as input will query the database to see if a file with the same attributes has already been stored. If this is the case, it will connect the already stored file with the current program execution, transitively connecting whatever has lead to the file with the current program execution. The attributes which are compared depend on the particular type of file.

On the more fine grained level, connecting the data items is done with the same handlers used to infer the hierarchy. These handlers tracking the hierarchy will also look up from which spectra a given peptide has been inferred. Clearly this process is based on additional information which is different for each handler. Making this connection between spectra and peptide is based on the same spectra identifier used in both files. All files processed in the TPP have for each data item unique identifiers allowing to connect data items before and after program execution.

14.2.5. Evolution of the TPP

The tools of the TPP are continuously released in new versions and the corresponding program in the TPP must be replaced. Also, additional tools may become available. Examples of such tools include additional programs to quantify proteins or peptides, alternative algorithms to identify proteins etc. Additional tools are likely to modify the structure, the sequence of execution of the TPP.

Having wrapped the TPP into a workflow makes it simpler to accommodate for these changes. Tools can easily be replaced and the workflow can be modified to execute new tools.

Possible changes, particularly to the structure of the workflow, also have an impact on the lineage information. Clearly, new tools need to be instrumented to provide the necessary lineage information. At the same time, the schema of the lineage information stored in the database may require changes which then again would require changes to the queries used to retrieve this information. Changes to schema and queries however cannot be made every time the workflow changes. Statically mapping the lineage information onto the schema is thus not a workable approach and an encoding of the information independent of the workflow structure has to be found.

14.3. Encoding Approaches

Given the query workload which consists of batches of queries about the hierarchy and dependency relationships between data and programs, an appropriate encoding for such interrelated data must be found. To store and retrieve the lineage information efficiently, we have evaluated several approaches that can deal with change, i.e., do not make any assumptions about the structure of the files and the lineage dependency graph. We consider two different types of queries, i.e., hierarchy queries and dependency queries working on different structures, trees for the former and DAGs for the latter. What we therefore need is an encoding for the transitive closure of trees and DAG so that they can be efficiently stored in a relational database and also be efficiently retrieved. We will evaluate encoding approaches for trees and DAGs separately.

14.3.1. Tree Encoding Approaches

We will first look at two different encodings for tree structures: recursive and interval encoding. The former can also be readily used for DAG structures while the latter cannot but it is the basis for a number of efficient encodings for DAGs as will be discussed later.

Recursive Queries

Existing systems used to record and retrieve lineage information [70, 4] store the tree or DAG as an adjacency list in the DB and use recursive queries to answer queries about the transitive closure. This approach has the advantage of being very fast when storing the information. In fact, for a tree $G = (V, E)$, the time to encode only depends on the number of edges $|E|$ as does the space required to store it.

Querying however may be costly, as queries need to be executed recursively. The runtime of such a recursive query depends on two factors, the number of recursion levels and the number of edges $|E|$. The former can grow up to the length of the tree, where the length is defined to be the longest directed path in the tree, which is at most equal to the number of edges $|E|$. For deep trees, such queries may not be very efficient.

Interval Encoding

Another tree encoding approach which has been used in several applications [32, 81, 112] is interval encoding which has already been discussed in Section 13.1.4.

Interval Assignment: The intervals of a tree can be assigned by traversing it. The left boundary value of the interval is assigned preorder and the right value postorder. This guarantees that the intervals are assigned to comply with the definitions outlined before. Encoding in the case of interval encoding means assigning intervals to nodes. In case of a *tree* this can be done by visiting all nodes and edges and the complexity therefore is linear with respect to the number of edges $|E|$ and vertices $|V|$ in the tree.

Querying: Answering the question about the lineage of a node, e.g., querying for all predecessors of a node, can be done by determining what interval (associated to a node) encloses this interval. Equally, finding all successors of a node can be done by testing what intervals are enclosed by the node.

The complexity for querying trees depends on the number of vertices $|V|$, hence the complexity of the query is $O(|V|)$.

14.3.2. DAG Encoding Approaches

As we have already discussed in Section 14.2, the lineage dependency information can be represented as a DAG. What we are interested in are queries over the transitive closure of the DAG. In particular, we want to support question such as what items did depend on other items in the protein inference, e.g., what peptides did the proteins depend on and so on. We also want to ask the question of impact, e.g. what proteins did this peptide or spectrum have an impact on. In other words, we want to retrieve all nodes that are reachable from one particular node (or a set of nodes) or we want to query for all nodes which reach a particular node.

The problem is related to the question of graph reachability. The question asked in graph reachability is, whether a node can be reached from another. When asking for the lineage of a node n, one asks for all nodes reachable form n. With minor modifications, graph reachability approaches can be used to answer the lineage question as well.

We have evaluated several approaches to store and retrieve data lineage, some designed for graph reachability and one used to answer lineage queries. All of the approaches tested are based on the interval assignment discussed for trees in discussed in the previous chapter in Section 13.1.4. Because intervals cannot be assigned to DAGs readily, one class of approaches uses additional lookup tables and more complex queries. A second type of approach modifies the graph to make it amenable to interval encoding. We have in particular compared the Dual Labeling (Dual-I & Dual-II), GRIPP, IDAG (as presented in Section 13.2) and the recursive approach. We have chosen the first three approaches for their comparatively low theoretical complexities in terms of encoding, retrieval time, and space. The recursive approach is included because it is the prevalent approach in lineage management systems. The complexity of updates for these approaches is not relevant as the lineage information is written once after the experiment is executed and it is not changed thereafter. In what follows we initially outline each of the approaches, discuss potential problems and illustrate them with measurements. The authors of the GRIPP and Dual approaches have kindly provided us with the code to run the experiments.

14. Sisyphus Use Case

Dual Labeling (Dual-I & Dual-II)

The dual labeling approach divides the edge set of the graph in two sets [120]. The first contains all edges of the spanning tree of the graph and the second set contains all remaining edges, the so called non-tree edges. The spanning tree is encoded with intervals. The non-tree edges are stored in a link table. Testing the reachability for two nodes involves checking reachability in the spanning tree and subsequently following the non-tree-edges in the link table. Querying the spanning tree is relatively fast, querying the link table however slows down the query. Whilst one can argue that, when testing for reachability, answers can often already be given by only querying the spanning tree, therefore reducing the average query time, this is not the case for the lineage query where the entire transitive closure of the graph must be explored.

Depending on how the link table is organized, queries can significantly be sped up. One such improvement is to not just store the non-tree edges but also additional edges representing the transitive reachability information of the non-tree edges. This significantly reduces the number of look ups in the link table. Two variants of Dual have been devised. Dual-II trades time for space by reducing the size of the link table to the adverse effect that queries are executed slower. The complexity of querying with Dual-II is O(log t) (t is the number of non-tree edges). Dual-I uses a bigger link table but can reduce the query complexity to O(1). Both approaches have the same theoretical complexity for encoding the graph.

Clearly, the performance can also be improved by minimizing the size of the link table which can be achieved through maximizing the spanning tree.

Implementation: The code provided by the authors of the approach calculates labels and the link table, stores both in data structures in main memory and queries over them. Because our application manages massive amounts of interrelated data, we cannot store the data in main memory but have to store it in a database. We therefore use the code of the authors [120] to calculate labels and the link table and then store the labels and links in tables in the database. We have used the C++ code from the authors to write the corresponding SQL query.

Discussion: This approach works particularly well for tree-like graphs, that is for sparse graphs where the number of non-tree edges t is very small compared with the number of edges in the graph. For denser graphs, however, the number of non-tree edges becomes big and contributes significantly to the overall complexity. We measured this behavior for increasingly dense DAGs. The graph density is measured as the ratio of edges to nodes (this is the non-normalized graph density [24]).

We have measured t in a series of experiments where we have left the number of vertices constant at 2000 but have varied the number of edges, ranging from 2000 to 15000. The results, plotting the graph density versus the number of non-tree edges, are shown in Figure 14.5.

As Figure 14.5 shows, the number of non-tree edges grows very fast. A big t is only problematic if it starts to dominate the complexity of the encoding, which has complexity $O(|V| + |E| + t^3)$ (for $G = (V, E)$). With t^3 this happens very soon. Clearly, as the

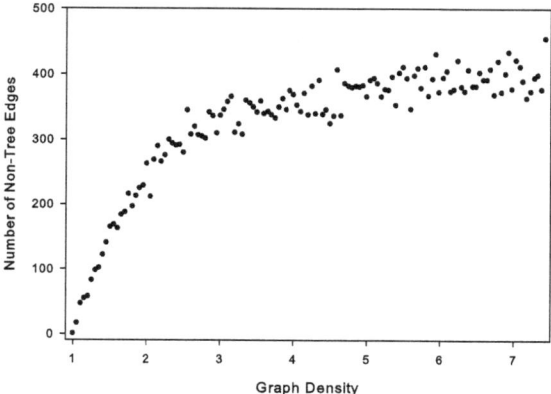

Figure 14.5.: Number of Non-tree edges for increasing graph density

authors of the approach point out, the approach is very well-suited for sparse tree-like graphs. It does not do well for denser graphs.

GRIPP

The GRIPP approach transforms the DAG into a tree in order to use interval encoding [111]. To compute this tree, the graph is traversed depth-first and intervals are assigned to the nodes. An edge over which a node is reached the first time is called tree-edge. All following edges to the same node are called non-tree edges. If a node is reached over a non-tree edge, its successors will not be visited. The node will be copied and the non-tree edge will now have the copied node as destination. Such a copied node is called a non-tree node and will also get an interval assigned. Copying the node and redirecting the edge will ensure that the in-degree of all nodes in the graph is at most one and the graph is in fact a tree. With G=(V,E), copying nodes will lead to a maximum of $|E|$ additional nodes, resulting in an overall space complexity of $O(|V|+|E|)$. Encoding of the graph can be done in a graph traversal in $O(|V|+|E|)$.

When testing if a node a is reachable from node b, it is first tested if the interval of b is in the interval of a. If the interval of a contains any non-tree node c, then a query testing if b is in the interval of c is executed. This is done recursively until b is found or the entire tree is traversed, leading to a worst case complexity of $O(|V|-|E|)$ queries. The number of non-tree nodes can be reduced by adjusting the traversal order with which the tree is built. An additional strategy for reducing the number of queries when querying for the lineage of node a is to avoid executing a query for a non-tree node n of

14. Sisyphus Use Case

which the reachable nodes are a subset of the reachable nodes of a. The authors of the approach claim that reducing the number of non-tree nodes which need to be queried leads to an almost constant number of queries needed to be executed.

The number of queries which need to be executed to retrieve the lineage of a node in the graph may grow big for large graphs. It depends on the number of non-tree nodes in the tree which in turn depends on the average in-degree of the nodes in the graph (every node is copied $n-1$ times to a non-tree node where n is the in-degree). To study the behavior of the approach we have generated random graphs with an increasing average in-degree of its nodes. The average in-degree of a graph is its non-normalized density. For each node we have retrieved its reachable nodes, i.e., its lineage and have measured the number of queries that need to be executed. The results are shown in Figure 14.6.

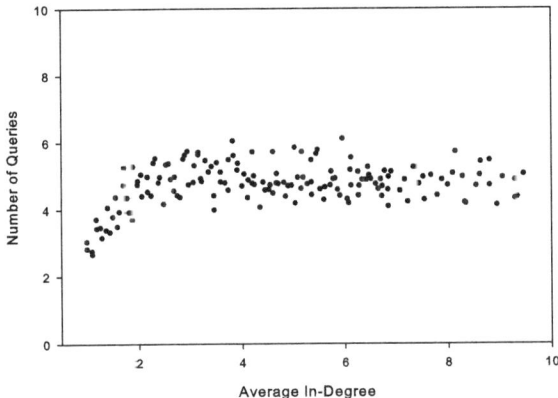

Figure 14.6.: Increasing number of queries for dense graphs

Even if the density of the graph increases, the number of queries required converges to the upper bound of 6 and generally remains between 4 and 6.

Implementation: We have used the PL/SQL code provided by the authors with minor modifications to implement this approach. The code defines several stored procedures for storing and retrieving the graph information. We have modified the procedure to retrieve graph information such that it does not test for reachability of two nodes, but instead traverses and returns the entire subtree reachable from node a, a being the node we want to know the lineage of.

Discussion: This approach has very interesting theoretical upper bounds for the time required for encoding and for the space for storing the information. Executing $O(|V| - |E|)$ queries for retrieving the lineage of just one node however may introduce unacceptable overhead. Even if the number of queries required to be executed in order to retrieve

14. Sisyphus Use Case

lineage information is almost constant, the overhead of executing these queries may still be high. The stored procedure executing these queries also maintains several temporary tables, writing and reading from them during execution. This is done in order to avoid querying the same interval range twice. While this also reduces the number of queries executed, it also introduces overhead and consequently executing the stored procedure once takes 1ms.

Interval Encoding for DAGs (IDAG)

Only the subset of DAGs which have a partial-order dimension of two or less [95] can be encoded with intervals. IDAG exploits this by transforming arbitrary DAGs into DAGs of partial-order dimension two if necessary. IDAG first tests if the partial-order dimension of the DAG is at most two. If this is the case, then the DAG can be directly encoded with intervals. If this is not the case, the DAG will be transformed in a DAG with equivalent transitive closure. To do this, each of the independent subgraphs is tested for its partial-order dimension and if this exceeds two, the subgraph is transformed to a transitive closure equivalent tree. To do so nodes are duplicated such that the reachability information in the tree is the same as in the subgraph. Trees can always be encoded with intervals and once a subgraph is transformed to a tree it replaces the subgraph in the graph. Once the partial-order dimension of the entire graph is two, the intervals are assigned to the nodes. The first two phases, testing for the partial-order dimension and transformation, can be executed in polynomial time with respect to the number of vertices and edges in the DAG, whereas the last phase is of linear complexity.

Implementation: To encode the fine-grained lineage as discussed before we have improved IDAG by reducing the complexity of the first phase, which ultimately reduces the overall complexity, particularly in case the second phase can be skipped. Instead of using the algorithm of polynomial complexity to test the partial order dimension [95] as it has been described in Section 13.2, we have implemented an approach which can test the DAG in linear time [110]. Our experiments indicate that the test phase is the most time consuming phase. Using a linear time algorithm greatly reduces overall execution time also when a transformation is necessary.

Discussion: This approach yields fast lookup times because only a very simple query has to be executed. The problem of this approach is however that it is difficult to assess if a transformation is necessary and, if so, how many nodes need to be duplicated. A transformation has a significant impact on the time required to encode as well as the space needed to store it. It may also have an adverse impact on the runtime of queries which, if the DAG has been transformed, have to be evaluated over more tuples.

To illustrate this problem, we have tried to determine on what the number of duplicated nodes depend and have tried to correlate this number with characteristics of the graph. Of all graph characteristics we have tested, the partial-order dimension seems to correlate best with the number of tuples duplicated. For randomly generated graphs, we have measured the ratio between the number of nodes in the DAG and the number of duplicated nodes versus the partial-order dimension of it. The results are shown in Figure 14.7.

14. Sisyphus Use Case

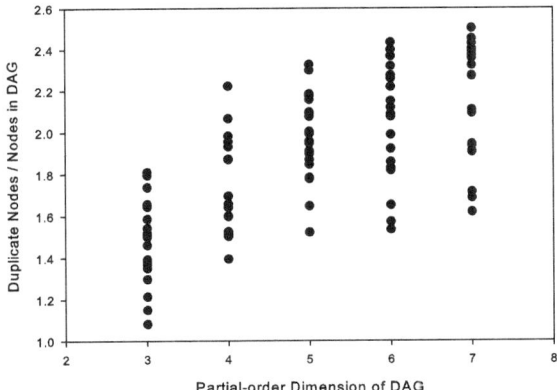

Figure 14.7.: Increase in tuples with increasing DAG dimension

Knowing the partial-order dimension helps assessing the number of tuples which need to be duplicated. Determining the dimension of a DAG is however difficult in practice, particularly for large graphs. The problem is NP-complete and for the measurements shown before, we have only been able to test for small graphs of up to 100 nodes.

It is thus difficult to determine how many nodes will be duplicated in order to encode a given graph with intervals. As we have shown in the previous chapter, randomly generated graphs seem to require significant transformation whereas lineage graphs resulting from real workflows are sufficiently simple and do not require much transformation if any at all.

14.4. Encoding Evaluation

In this section we first compare and evaluate the recursive and interval encoding approaches for tree structure in case of hierarchy queries. We then discuss performance evaluations comparing GRIPP, Dual-I & II and IDAG for encoding & retrieving dependency information.

The setup used was the same throughout all experiments: two nodes in a cluster of Linux machines (dual Opteron 2.4 GHz machines with 2 GB memory) connected with a 1Gb/s local area network. One node hosted a Oracle 11g database where the graph information was stored while the other node hosted the client. The client performed the encoding in all cases except for GRIPP and issued all queries. In the case of GRIPP, the encoding was executed on the server as this approach is implemented as a number

14. Sisyphus Use Case

of stored procedures. To retrieve the information in case of the recursive approach also stored procedures were used.

14.4.1. Hierarchy Queries

In this section we discuss storing and retrieving hierarchical information, i.e., tree information from the XML structures of the files storing proteins, peptides etc. We measure the size of such trees in the number of vertices they contain and generate random trees with a maximum depth of 4. A typical size of such a tree in the experiments is 5000 vertices with a depth of up to 4.

Storing

A first experiment carried out compares the time required by both approaches to store the hierarchical lineage information, i.e. the tree structure. Figure 14.8 depicts the time required for both approaches relative to the tree size measured in the number of vertices. As can be seen, the time required for both approaches grows linear with the tree size.

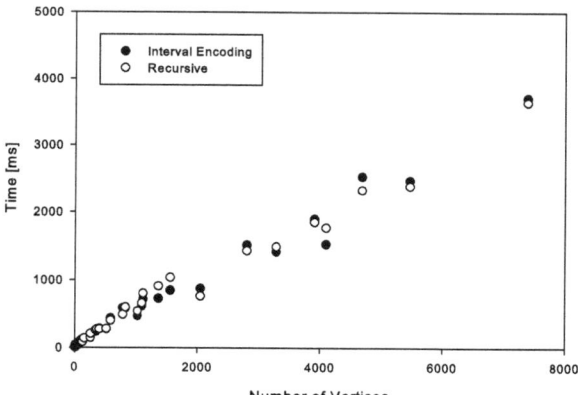

Figure 14.8.: Storing hierarchical information

The process of storing the hierarchical information of the trees is different for the two approaches. In case of the recursive approach, the node IDs and their parent IDs have to be stored in no particular order. For storing the information with interval encoding, the intervals need to be calculated first which can be done by traversing the tree depth-first. The slightly more complex procedure of encoding the tree with the interval encoding results in only slightly higher times.

14. Sisyphus Use Case

For both approaches, storing a typical protXML file with 5000 vertices takes between 1.5 and 1.6 seconds.

Querying

Two different queries are relevant in the context of the hierarchical structure. The first query asks about the membership of an item, e.g., in what protXML file is this protein stored. Answering such questions amounts to querying up the tree structure. We have measured the time it takes to execute such a query depending on the size of the tree, i.e., the XML file. Figure 14.9 compares the two approaches for such a query. A random leaf node was repeatedly chosen and the root of the tree it is member of was retrieved.

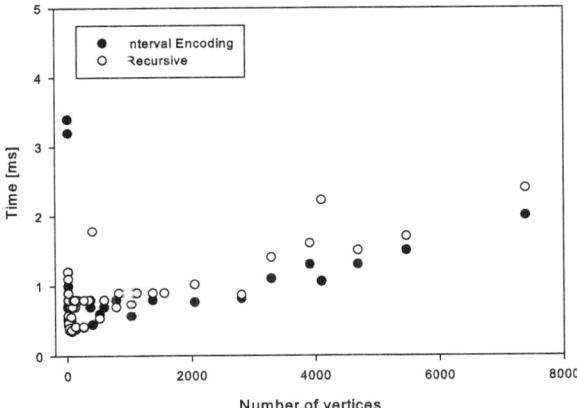

Figure 14.9.: Querying up the hierarchical information

As can be seen, the difference for both approaches is small. For a file with 5000 vertices, the time is between 1.5 and 1.8 ms.

The second query may for instance retrieve all proteins in a given file, or the proteins in a particular protein group, etc. and therefore queries down the hierarchical structure of the tree. Figure 14.10 compares the two approaches with a growing size of the tree. For this series of experiments the root was selected and all its children were queried for.

The two approaches differ significantly, with the recursive approach growing much faster than the interval approach. While for the query in the case of the interval approach only the number of stored vertices matter, for the recursive approach the numbers of paths which need to be followed matter. The number of paths is equal to the number of leaf nodes in the tree. For an example file, the number of leafs is 5000 and the number

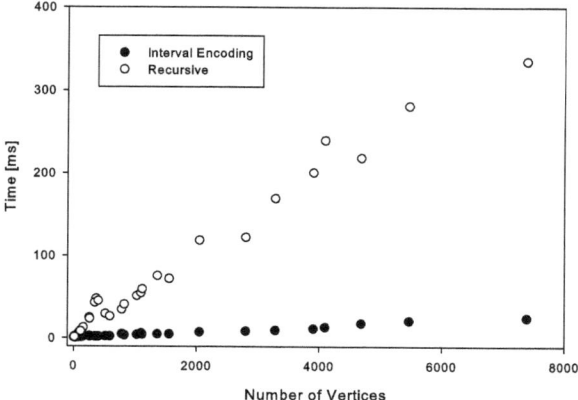

Figure 14.10.: Querying down the hierarchical information

of paths 5000. This leads to a time of 4.8ms in case of the interval approach and of 75.9ms for the recursive approach.

Space

The space required to store the tree structure matches the theoretical complexity for both approaches. In case of the recursive approach this is the number of edges in the tree. For the interval encoding approach it is the number of vertices.

Discussion

Both approaches have similar complexities with respect to time to encode/store and space. The major difference however is in retrieving child nodes where interval encoding is significantly faster and scales better. Retrieving child nodes is an important aspect of the encoding approach for our application where many queries will for instance be issued to ask for the children of a spectrum.

14.4.2. Dependency Queries

In order to answer dependency queries, the lineage information has to be retrieved from the TPP. This is done by parsing the XML files involved in the TPP and linking these items together by using unique identifiers. This relationship information is represented with a DAG.

Graph Structure

The lineage graph of one experiment has as nodes the proteins, peptides, parameters, spectras etc. which are part of the experiment. In it, two nodes are connected with a directed edge if the source node has had an impact on the destination node. The sinks in the graph are the proteins, being at the end of the protein inference process and items, such as parameters, database entries, spectras etc. are roots at the begin of the identification process.

For our application, we need to be able to ask queries in both directions, e.g., what has had an influence on this protein inference and on what did this peptide have an influence. We are thus querying for the lineage of proteins, requesting all items which had an influence on it and on the other hand we ask for the impact of, e.g., a spectra, asking on what peptide or protein did this spectra have an impact.

Asking both questions about lineage and impact of items is not a problem for IDAG and the recursive approach. One can ask what intervals are contained in this node's interval, for asking the question what does this node have an influence on. Asking what did have an influence on a given node can then be done by asking what intervals do contain the node's interval. For the recursive approach we have to provide a second stored procedure querying recursively up the graph.

There is however no similar solution for the Dual and GRIPP approaches. Consequently, we store the graph structure twice, flipping the direction of the edges when storing it the second time. This has an influence on the time required to encode as well as on the space. We did however not include this in the measurements for storage space and time to encode.

Storing

In this series of experiments we have measured the time it takes to store example experiments of increasing sizes (measured in terms of protein inferences) in the database. Storing the experiment includes encoding the DAG and storing it in the database. The results are depicted in Figure 14.11.

In case of the recursive approach the adjacency list containing all edges needs to be stored. Consequently, the space required is linear with the number of edges $|E|$.

Both Dual approaches have a theoretical complexity of $O(|V - |E| + t^3)$ for the encoding step with t being the number of the non-tree edges. In case of the lineage graph from an experiment with 1000 protein inferences, the number of such edges is 9045. This of course contributes significantly to the time required to encode as has already been discussed in Section 14.3.2. Consequently the time to store the lineage information for both Dual approaches is high. Dual-II seems to be slightly slower which is due to the additional calculations needed to reduce the size of the data structure.

The GRIPP approach does much better. However even though the theoretical bound is only $O(|V| + |E|)$, the time required is still substantial. This is due to the additional improvements which go beyond the simple construction of the tree as discussed in Section 14.3.2.

14. Sisyphus Use Case

Clearly, the IDAG approach benefits from the comparatively simple structure of the DAG. Only few transformations are required, resulting in 19'921 duplicated nodes for an experiment of size 1000. If the structure of the graph was more intricate, more transformations would be required, requiring more time to encode. With the current structure of the DAG however, the overall time is comparatively low. Even though the time to encode is of polynomial complexity in case of this approach, the results indicate an almost linear behavior.

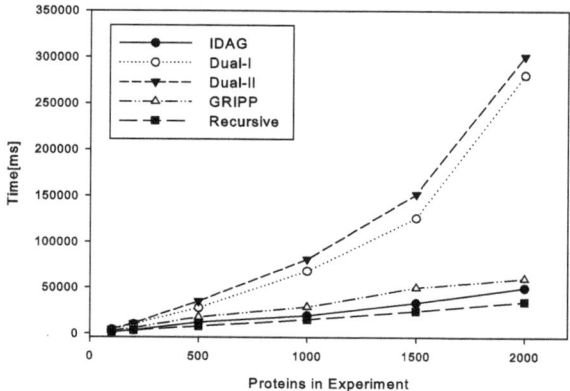

Figure 14.11.: Time to store experiments

Querying

We have measured with each encoding approach the time required to retrieve the lineage information of a batch of 1000 items. This is a very common query, for instance when retrieving the lineage of soluble proteins in an experiment or a group of proteins sharing a different attribute.

We have measured both the time required to query for the lineage of proteins, find what spectras lead to their inference, and what proteins have been inferred from a given spectra. The results are depicted in Figure 14.12.

The recursive approaches needs the most time to retrieve the lineage of the batch of proteins with roughly 4400ms in both directions. The stored procedure implementing this approach needs to be executed over 7 levels of recursion in both directions and hence the time required is roughly the same in either case.

GRIPP requires less time than the recursive approach but substantially more than the other approaches. The stored procedure for the GRIPP approach is quite complex

14. Sisyphus Use Case

and requires the recursive execution of queries. The number of recursions does depend on the average in-degree of the nodes in the graph as has been illustrated in Section 14.3.2. When encoding the graph for asking about the lineage of proteins, the average in-degree of nodes is 2.36 whereas it is 2.91 when encoding for asking about the impact of spectras. This difference explains the noticeable difference in the execution times for queries in the two directions.

Both Dual approaches have similar queries for retrieving the lineage as does IDAG. The dual query first queries over the transitive closure of the spanning tree of the graph and in a second step over the link table. The query for IDAG on the other hand only has to query of the transitive closure of the modified graph. The lower complexity of the query for IDAG explains that it is slightly faster. Flipping the edges in case of the Dual approach in order to encode for queries in both directions leads to a different number of non-tree nodes for the experiment as has been reported previously with 8816 edges. This difference of non-tree nodes is however not noticeable.

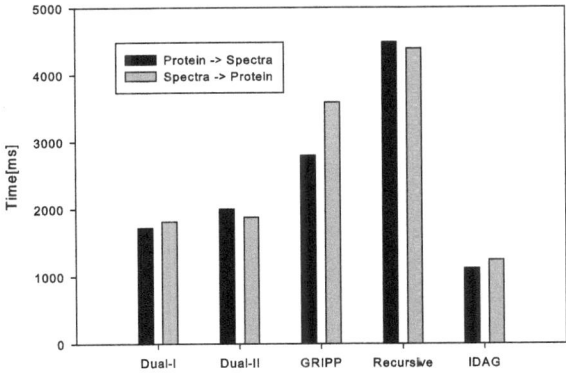

Figure 14.12.: Time to retrieve dependency information

Space

We have also measured the space required to store the lineage information for the different approaches and experiments of different size as is depicted in Figure 14.13. This is a particular interesting experiment for the Dual-I and II as well as IDAG as they do not have strict upper bounds for the space complexity. The other two approaches on the other hand behave as is to be expected. The recursive approach requires $|E|$ tuples to store all edges. GRIPP needs slightly less than the theoretical upper bound of $O(|V| + |E|)$ and also grows linearly.

14. Sisyphus Use Case

The Dual approaches again suffer from the high number of non-tree edges and require the most space, significantly more than the others. Dual-II trades time for space and requires less space for storing the information. Both are however not as high as their analytical upper bound. But with an increasing size of the experiment and therewith with an increasing size of the lineage DAG, the number of non-tree edges grows and the t term of the space complexity $O(|V| + t^2)$ lets the number of tuples grow fast.

Surprisingly, IDAG does not require excessive space and also grows near linearly for an increasing experiment size. As has been mentioned earlier, 19921 nodes in the DAG need to be duplicated for an experiment of size 1000, putting this approach behind GRIPP and recursive but clearly ahead of Dual.

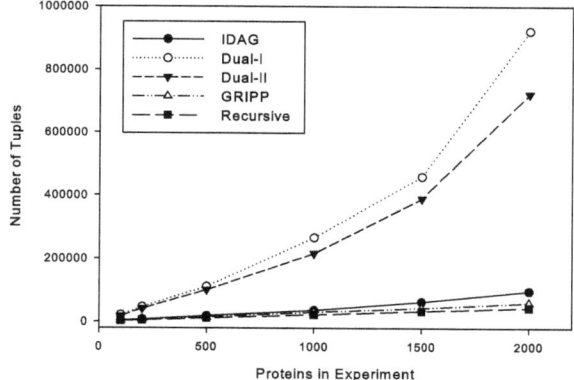

Figure 14.13.: Space needed to store one experiment

Discussion

The most important property for our application is the time required to execute dependency queries. When comparing the approaches, the time to retrieve the lineage of just one protein differs only in the order of few milliseconds. In our application queries for retrieving the lineage of a batch of proteins are very frequent. In case of such batches which retrieve the lineage of hundreds or thousands of proteins, milliseconds translate into seconds and start to make a difference.

Choosing the right encoding for the dependency information is not trivial. Depending on the structure of the lineage DAG, different encoding approaches may suit best. If the DAG was tree like, with a low number of non-tree edges, Dual-I or Dual-II may suit best. In case the DAG was significantly more intricate, the GRIPP approach may provide the best performance by having a constant number of queries to be executed.

14. Sisyphus Use Case

The DAG structure in our case however is not tree-like, but also does not seem to have a high partial-order dimension making the modified IDAG approach most suitable. This approach trades space for time and with an increase of the number of tuples required to be stored, this approach has the lowest time to retrieve the information. Even if IDAG is only slightly faster than Dual and GRIPP, it clearly outperforms both when encoding the DAG and stores the lineage information without an undue penalty regarding space.

We thus consider IDAG to be the most suitable encoding approach for dependency queries in our application. It is very efficient with respect to storing and retrieving the dependency graph and is also reasonable regarding space. It supports both types of queries, lineage and impact, without any changes.

14.5. Sisyphus

We have implemented the modified IDAG approach and the interval encoding approach in Sisyphus. The goal of Sisyphus is to enable users to manage cell surface proteomic experiments results. It directly integrates the TPP and hence allows the user to import raw experiment data over which the TPP tools are run subsequently. Upon experiment import, annotation information is imported automatically. All information, from experiment results and annotations, is stored in a database. The information is made available through a Web frontend accessible through the browser. With this the users are able to search and manage experiments as well as retrieve the lineage of entire experiments or more fine-granular data like proteins, spectras etc.

To enable this, the lineage information is captured, encoded and stored at the end of the data processing with the TPP. The time required to execute the TPP depends on the size of the raw experiment data processed, the input parameters and the size of the reference database searched. For an experiment with 4000 spectras in the raw input data and one database searched, the running time is between 5 and 7 minutes. Storing the dependency information takes an additional 20 seconds and storing the hierarchy information takes 18 seconds for all files processed. Storing the information thus adds 38 seconds, increasing the overall time to run an experiment between 9% and 12%.

Because the two approaches for storing hierarchical information do not differ significantly, the only way to speed up the storing process is to switch to the recursive approach for the dependency information. This is the fastest approach for storing & encoding the dependency information and using it would reduce the overall time to 34 seconds. This only reduces the time to store the lineage information by 11%.

Accepting this 11% time penalty for encoding however allows a question like 'Retrieve the lineage of all protein with a probability bigger than 90% in a specific experiment?' to be answered substantially faster. The question queries for the lineage of ca. 500 proteins in 0.7s instead of 3.7s when using the recursive approach to store the dependency information. With the encoding chosen, similarly significant speedups can be achieved for many batch queries which are very frequent in Sisyphus. Such speed ups contribute considerably to the usability of Sisyphus.

15. Conclusions

The ability to track lineage is of paramount importance for scientific applications. Without being able to track back the origin of a given data set, no conclusive statement can be made about it, rendering it virtually useless. Several different systems have been implemented to track the lineage of individual data sets, however, none of them focuses on the efficient storage and retrieval of lineage information. They instead use recursive queries, which do not scale for very large workflows as we have shown.

In Chapter 13, we have presented an alternative approach for storing the transitive closure of dependency graphs of data sets and tasks. The new approach transforms, if necessary, an arbitrary graph into an interval encodable graph while maintaining the transitive closure, encodes it and stores it in the database. As the evaluation on coarse-grained, workflow-based lineage information demonstrates, this encoding allows for very fast lineage queries over the transitive closure for a wide range of workflow types without imposing an undue penalty in terms of storage.

Storing only coarse-grained, file based lineage and making it available to scientists however is in many cases not enough for them to ask sophisticated lineage questions. With the example of proteomics experiments and the TPP processing pipeline, we have shown in Chapter 14 how to exploit structured files passed between the tools of the TPP in order to access fine-grained lineage. Collecting fine-grained lineage challenges current methods of encoding graph structures. For our application which processes the data with the TPP, we have evaluated encoding approaches for hierarchy as well as dependency information. With the initial discussion and the evaluation we have shown that choosing the right encoding has a significant impact on the performance of lineage queries. The performance depends on the characteristics of the graph that represents the dependency information.

In the case of the lineage generated by our processing pipeline, the modified IDAG approach suited best as it is the fastest to retrieve dependency information. It surprisingly did not require much time to encode and also not as much space as expected. Given the specific structure of the graph, with many non-tree edges, both Dual approaches did not perform well regarding time to encode and the space needed. The recursive approach was very fast for encoding and requires the least space. In our experiments it was however the slowest approach when querying for lineage information. GRIPP also required little space but did not perform well regarding encoding and retrieving information. If the lineage graph had a significant higher partial-order dimension, the GRIPP approach may be faster to retrieve dependency information as its retrieval time is constant.

For the hierarchy information, we have evaluated the interval encoding and the recursive approach. Both approaches behave similarly for all queries except for the those

15. Conclusions

retrieving the children of a node. In this case, the difference for the two approaches is in the order of milliseconds when querying for many children.

We have implemented IDAG for dependency information and interval encoding for hierarchy information in Sisyphus. Lineage related queries can be answered significantly faster with it, improving the usability of Sisyphus significantly.

16. Conclusions

eScience, supporting researchers in traditional sciences by providing them with computational tools, has become a reality. An increasing number of scientific disciplines already use computational tools to process and organize raw experiment data obtained from instruments. Building and running these tools as well as managing the results however is by far not simple and requires adequate infrastructure to build upon. Building such infrastructure is challenging and has opened many research questions.

In this book we have addressed three specific problems in building such infrastructure. In the first part we have addressed the problem of publishing and sharing workflows implementing data processing pipelines. Publishing and letting other scientists use developed workflows has become a very important aspect of scientific communication. To enable this, workflows must be given an appropriate interface. Some known approaches provide workflows with proprietary interfaces, making their integration into other applications inherently difficult. Other approaches provide the workflow with a Web service interface. While this makes it simpler to integrate it, it does only insufficiently model the state a workflow execution, as a Web service is not stateful. This is a problem as scientific workflows typically are long running and maintain state.

For this reason we have defined a mapping between workflows and the Web Service Resource Framework (WS-RF) and Notifications (WS-N) standards for stateful services. This mapping provides workflows with a standardized interface, significantly simplifying their reuse and integration into other workflows, applications and portals. With this interface, computations modeled as a workflow can be initiated, monitored, steered, suspended and resumed remotely.

We have also reported on implementing this mapping, considering two different architectures. A first architectural approach adds an additional layer on top the workflow execution engine and mirrors all state of the underlying workflow execution in this layer. This additional layer makes querying for the state of the workflow execution fast, unfortunately however at the cost of constantly having to update the mirrored state. The second approach translates incoming client requests from the standardized WS-RF interface to the engine API. The experimental evaluation of the two approaches has shown that the second approach scales much better than the first. As opposed to the first approach, in case of the second approach, synchronization can be done on a much more fine-grained level, on the level of workflow executions. With this the second approach can manage the lifecycle of hundreds of thousands of workflow executions.

The second part addressed applying autonomic computing principles to simplify the deployment and the maintenance of a execution engine for heterogeneous workloads of scientific workflows. We have first described how to, by using JOpera, replicate the functionality of a workflow execution engine across a cluster. We have subsequently

16. Conclusions

described and implemented an autonomic controller which monitors the distributed engine. By monitoring the behavior of the engine, this controller will detect if the engine is properly configured for the currently executed workload. If this is not the case, it will reconfigure it on the fly. The controller also takes failures into account and adapts the engine configuration accordingly.

The behavior of the controller can be configured with policies. Not only can these policies define how to grow or shrink the system depending on the size of the workload but they also define how to reconfigure it according to the characteristics of the workload. With these policies we have been able to show that autonomic reconfiguration of the execution engine at runtime in our experiments outperforms manual configuration.

Although the controller relieves an administrator from configuring the system, the basic policies devised first did require configuration themselves. Configuring the autonomic controller however is a difficult problem in itself and we have thus developed further policies by removing any need for configuration. We have first developed a policy based on a PID controller. Even though this policy still needs to be configured, setting these parameters properly is well documented in the literature. To remove any need of configuration we have in a final step developed a zero-configuration policy based on an analytical model of the system. Removing any need for manual configuration, the latter two policies provide a substantial performance gain over the basic policies.

In the third part we have studied the problem of tracking and storing the lineage information for efficient retrieval. Storing the lineage information when processing data in workflows is essential. Without knowing the origin of the data, what raw experiment data was used, what programs were used to process the data, data products can neither be reproduced nor be understood. Using workflows to process the data makes it significantly simpler to record this information as the workflow can be understood as a recipe for processing the data.

Storing this information however is still a difficult problem. Current methods for storing such information do not scale well. Systems to manage, store and retrieve lineage information still use recursive queries which for large graphs, can lead to unacceptable high response times when answering lineage queries. We have therefore developed a new method to encode lineage information which can be represented by directed acyclic graphs. The method builds on the very efficient interval encoding. This encoding yields very efficient lookup times and also requires very little space but it can unfortunately not be used for arbitrary DAGs. We have thus defined the algorithms required to transform any DAG into a DAG which can be encoded with intervals. Clearly such a transformation must preserve the transitive closure of the DAG, e.g. the information what tools and what data has been used to derive a given data set.

We have applied this transformation to lineage information DAGs produced by the execution of different scientific workflows. The new encoding clearly outperformed the encodings currently used in lineage management systems, without imposing an undue penalty regarding space to store and time to encode. We have also applied our method to store more fine-grained lineage obtained from biological experiments. Making such fine-grained lineage available is of great use to biologists. We have discussed how to retrieve such information from the workflows processing the raw experiment data and have compared our encoding to others when storing such information. Even for the large DAGs representing this fine-grained lineage information our approach to the problem did outperform known approaches.

Bibliography

[1] pyGridWare: Python Web Services Resource Framework. http://dsd.lbl.gov/gtg/projects/pyGridWare/. 7

[2] WSRF::Lite - A WSRF Implementation in Perl. http://www.sve.man.ac.uk/Research/AtoZ/ILCT. 7

[3] D. Abramson, J. Giddy, and L. Kotler. High Performance Parametric Modeling with Nimrod/G: Killer Application for the Global Grid? . In *IPDPS 2000: Proceedings of the 14th International Parallel and Distributed Processing Symposium*, 2000. 10

[4] P. Agrawal, O. Ben_elloun, A. D. Sarma, C. Hayworth, S. Nabar, T. Sugihara, and J. Widom. Trio: A System for Data, Uncertainty, and Lineage. In *VLDB '06: Proceedings of the 32nd International Conference on Very Large Data Bases*, 2006. 80, 82, 111

[5] G. Alonso, W. Bausch, C. Pautasso, and A. Kahn. Dependable Computing in Virtual Laboratories. In *ICDE '01: Proceedings of the 17th International Conference on Data Engineering*, 2001. 31, 80

[6] G. Alonso, F. Casati, H. Kuno, and V. Machiraju. *Web services: Concepts, Architectures and Applications*. Springer, November 2003. 31

[7] I. Altintas, C. Berkley, E. Jaeger, M. Jones, B. Ludascher, and S. Mock. Kepler: An Extensible System for Design and Execution of Scientific Workflows. In *SSDBM '04: Proceedings of the 16th International Conference on Scientific and Statistical Database Management*, June 2004. 31, 80

[8] R. Baird, M. Hepner, R. Gamble, and M. T. Gamble. Reconfiguring Workflows of Web Services. In *ICCBSS '07: Proc. of the Sixth International IEEE Conference on Commercial-off-the-Shelf (COTS)-Based Software Systems*, 2007. 34

[9] T. Bauer and P. Dadam. A Distributed Execution Environment for Large-Scale Workflow Management Systems with Subnets and Server Migration. In *CoopIS'97: Proceedings of the 2nd IFCIS International Conference on Cooperative Information Systems*, 1997. 31, 33

[10] A. Bergou, B. Berriman, E. Deelman, J. Good, J. C. Jacob, D. S. Katz, C. Kesselman, A. Laity, T. Prince, G. Singh, M.-H. Su, and R. Williams. Montage: A Grid Enabled Image Mosaic Service for the National Virtual Observatory. In *ADASS*

Bibliography

XIII: *Proceedings of the 13th Astronomical Data Analysis Software and Systems Conference*, 2003. 83, 101

[11] D. Bhagwat, L. Chiticariu, W.-C. Tan, and G. Vijayvargiya. An Annotation Management System for Relational Databases. In *VLDB '04: Proceedings of the 30st International Conference on Very Large Data Bases*, 2004. 82

[12] O. Biton, S. Cohen-Boulakia, S. Davidson, and C. Hara. Querying and Managing Provenance through User Views in Scientific Workflows. In *ICDE '08: Proceedings of the 24th IEEE International Conference on Data Engineering*, 2008. 82

[13] R. Bose and J. Frew. Lineage Retrieval for Scientific Data Processing: A Survey. *ACM Computing Survey*, 37(1):1–28, 2005. 80

[14] S. Bowers, T. M. McPhillips, and B. Ludäscher. Provenance in Collection-Oriented Scientific Workflows. *Concurrency and Computation: Practice & Experience*, 20(5):519–529, 2008. 107

[15] D. Breitgand, E. Henis, and O. Shehory. Automated and Adaptive Threshold Setting: Enabling Technology for Autonomy and Self-Management. In *ICAC '05: Proceedings of the Second International Conference on Automatic Computing*, 2005. 32, 33

[16] P. Buneman, S. Khanna, and W. C. Tan. Data Provenance: Some Basic Issues. In *FST TCS 2000: Proceedings of the 20th Conference on Foundations of Software Technology and Theoretical Computer Science*, 2000. 80

[17] P. Buneman, S. Khanna, and W.-C. Tan. Why and Where: A Characterization of Data Provenance. In *ICDT 2001: 8th International Database Theory Conference*, 2001. 80

[18] S. P. Callahan, J. Freire, E. Santos, C. E. Scheidegger, C. T. Silva, and H. T. Vo. Managing the Evolution of Dataflows with VisTrails. In *SciFlow 2006: Proceedings of IEEE Workshop on Workflow and Data Flow for Scientific Applications*, 2006. 82, 107

[19] J. Cao, S. A. Jarvis, S. Saini, and G. R. Nudd. GridFlow: Workflow Management for Grid Computing. In *CCGrid03: Proceedings of the 3rd International Symposium on Cluster Computing and the Grid*, 2003. 8, 31

[20] F. Casati and M.-C. Shan. Dynamic and Adaptive Composition of e-Services. *Information Systems*, 26:143–163, 2001. 5, 31

[21] G. Chafle, S. Chandra, V. Mann, and M. G. Nanda. Decentralized Orchestration of Composite Web Services. In *WWW '04: Proceedings of the 13th World Wide Web Conference*, 2004. 32, 33

Bibliography

[22] S. Cheshire and D. Steinberg. *Zero Configuration Networking: The Definitive Guide.* O'Reilly, 2005. 33

[23] W. Chrabakh and R. Wolski. GridSAT: A Chaff-based Distributed SAT Solver for the Grid. In *SC '03: Proceedings of the 2003 ACM/IEEE Conference on Supercomputing*, 2003. 83

[24] T. F. Coleman and J. J. More. Estimation of Sparse Jacobian Matrices and Graph Coloring Problems. *SIAM Journal on Numerical Analysis*, 20(1):187–209, 1983. 113

[25] P. Cominos and N. Munro. PID Controllers: Recent Tuning Methods and Design to Specification. *IEEE Proceedings on Control Theory and Applications*, 149(1):46–53, 2002. 66

[26] R. Craig and R. C. Beavis. TANDEM: Matching Proteins with Tandem Mass Spectra. *Bioinformatics*, 20(9):1466–1467, 2004. 105

[27] Y. Cui and J. Widom. Practical Lineage Tracing in Data Warehouses. In *ICDE '00: Proceedings of the 16th International Conference on Data Engineering*, 2000. 80

[28] Y. Cui, J. Widom, and J. L. Wiener. Tracing the Lineage of View Data in a Warehousing Environment. *ACM Transactions on Database Systems*, 25(2):179–227, 2000. 82

[29] K. Czajkowski, D. F. Ferguson, I. Foster, J. Frey, S. Graham, T. Maguire, D. Snelling, and S. Tuecke. From Open Grid Services Infrastructure to WSResource Framework: Refactoring & Evolution, 2002. http://www.globus.org/wsrf/specs/ogsi_to_wsrf_1.0.pdf. 7, 9

[30] K. Czajkowski, D. F. Ferguson, I. Foster, J. Frey, S. Graham, I. Sedukhin, D. Snelling, S. Tuecke, and W. Vambenepe. The WS-Resource Framework, June 2005. http://www.globus.org/wsrf/specs/ws-wsrf.pdf. 5, 9

[31] E. Deelman, J. Blythe, Y. Gil, and C. Kesselman. Workflow Management in GriPhyN. 2004. 8

[32] D. DeHaan, D. Toman, M. P. Consens, and M. T. Özsu. A Comprehensive XQuery to SQL Translation using Dynamic Interval Encoding. In *SIGMOD '03: Proceedings of the 28th ACM SIGMOD International Conference on Management of Data*, 2003. 86, 111

[33] B. Dushnik and E. W. Miller. Partially Ordered Sets. *American Journal of Mathematics*, 63:600–610, 1941. 88

[34] S. Even, A. Pnueli, and A. Lempel. Permutation Graphs and Transitive Graphs. *Journal of the ACM*, 19(3):400–410, 1972. 88

Bibliography

[35] T. Fahringer, J. Qin, and S. Hainzer. Specification of Grid Workflow Applications with AGWL: An Abstract Grid Workflow Language. In *CCGrid '05: Proceedings of Cluster Computing and the Grid*, 2005. 8

[36] I. Foster and C. Kesselman. Globus: A Metacomputing Infrastructure Toolkit. *The International Journal of Supercomputer Applications and High Performance Computing*, 11(2):115–128, 1997. 6, 7

[37] I. Foster, C. Kesselman, J. Nick, and S. Tuecke. The Physiology of the Grid: An Open Grid Services Architecture for Distributed Systems Integration. Technical report, Service Infrastructure Workgroup, Global Grid Forum, 2002. http://www.globus.org/research/papers/ogsa.pdf. 7

[38] I. Foster, S. Parastatidis, P. Watson, and M. Mckeown. How Do I Model State?: Let Me Count the Ways. *Commununications of the ACM*, 51(9):34–41, 2008. 5

[39] D. Georgakopoulos, M. F. Hornick, and A. P. Sheth. An Overview of Workflow Management: From Process Modelling to Workflow Automation Infrastructure. *Distributed and Parallel Databases*, 3(2):119–153, April 1995. 35

[40] M. Gillmann, W. Wonner, and G. Weikum. Workflow Management with Service Quality Guarantees. In *SIGMOD '02: Proceedings of the 27th ACM SIGMOD International Conference on Management of Data*, 2002. 33

[41] C. Goble, C. Wroe, and R. Stevens. Grid Project: Services, Architecture and Demonstrator, 2003. http://www.nesc.ac.uk/events/ahm2003/AHMCD/pdf/128.pdf. 7

[42] M. C. Golumbic and E. R. Scheinerman. Containment Graphs, Posets, and related Classes of Graphs. In *4ICC '89: Proceedings of the 3rd International Conference on Combinatorial Mathematics*, 1989. 88

[43] S. Graham, A. Karmarkar, J. Mischkinsky, I. Robinson, and I. Sedukhin. Web Services Resource 1.2, June 2005. http://docs.oasis-open.org/wsrf/wsrf-ws$_r esource-1.2-spec-pr-01.pdf.$ 9

[44] S. Graham and B. Murray. Web Services Base Notification 1.2, 2004. http://docs.oasis-open.org/wsn/2004/06/wsn-WS-BaseNotification-1.2-draft-03.pdf. 9, 24

[45] S. Graham and J. Treadwell. Web Services Resource Properties 1.2, June 2004. http://docs.oasis-open.org/wsrf/wsrf-ws_resource_properties-1.2-spec-pr-01.pdf. 9

[46] S. Harizopoulos and A. Ailamaki. A Case for Staged Database Systems. In *CIDR '03: Proceedings of the First First Biennial Conference on Innovative Data Systems Research*, 2003. 33

Bibliography

[47] T. Heinis and G. Alonso. Efficient Lineage Tracking for Scientific Workflows. In *SIGMOD '08: Proceedings of the 33rd ACM SIGMOD International Conference on Management of Data*, 2008. 2, 80

[48] T. Heinis and C. Pautasso. Automatic Configuration of an Autonomic Controller: An Experimental Study with Zero-Configuration Policies. In *ICAC '08: Proceedings of the 2008 International Conference on Autonomic Computing*, 2008. 2, 32

[49] T. Heinis, C. Pautasso, and G. Alonso. Design and Evaluation of an Autonomic Workflow Engine. In *ICAC '05: Proceedings of the Second International Conference on Automatic Computing*, 2005. 2, 31

[50] T. Heinis, C. Pautasso, and G. Alonso. Mirroring Resources or Mapping Requests: Implementing WS-RF for Grid Workflows. In *CCGrid '06: Proceedings of the Sixth IEEE International Symposium on Cluster Computing and the Grid*, 2006. 2, 6

[51] T. Heinis, C. Pautasso, O. Deak, and G. Alonso. Publishing Persistent Grid Computations as WS Resources. In *e-Science '05: Proceedings of the First International Conference on e-Science and Grid Computing*, 2005. 2, 5

[52] P. Heinl and H. Schuster. Towards a Highly Scaleable Architecture for Workflow Management Systems. In *DEXA '96: Proceedings of the 7th International Workshop on Database and Expert Systems Applications*, 1996. 33

[53] J. L. Hellerstein, Y. Diao, S. Parekh, and D. M Tilbury. *Feedback Control of Computing Systems*. John Wiley & Sons, 2004. 32, 65

[54] J. D. V. Horn. Online Availability of fMRI Results Images. *Journal of Cognitive Neuroscience*, 15(6):769–770, 2003. 73, 83, 100

[55] M. Humphrey, G. Wasson, K. Jackson, J. Boverhof, M. Rodriguez, J. Bester, J. Gawor, S. Lang, I Foster, S. Meder, S. Pickles, and M. McKewon. State and Events for Web Services: A Comparison of Five WS-Resource Framework and WS-Notification Implementations. In *HPDC 14: Proceedings of the 14th IEEE International Symposium on High Performance Distributed Computing*, 2005. 7, 16

[56] M. Humphrey, G. Wasson, M. Morgan, and N. Beekwilder. An Early Evaluation of WSRF and WS-Notification via WSRF.NET. In *Grid Computing Workshop '04 (associated with Supercomputing 2004)*, 2004. 7

[57] IBM. *TSpaces*. http://www.almaden.ibm.com/cs/TSpaces/. 38

[58] IBM. Autonomic Computing: Special Issue. *IBM Systems Journal*, 42(1), 2003. 33

Bibliography

[59] L. jie Jin, F. Casati, M. Sayal, and M.-C. Shan. Load Balancing in Distributed Workflow Management System. In *SAC '01: Proceedings of the 16th ACM Symposium on Applied Computing*, 2001. 31, 33

[60] N. Kandasamy, S. Abdelwahed, and J. P. Hayes. Self-Optimization in Computer Systems via Online Control: Application to Power Management. In *ICAC '04: Proceedings of the 1st International Conference on Autonomic Computing*, 2005. 33

[61] J. Kephart. Research Challenges of Autonomic Computing. In *ICSE '05: Proceedings of the 27th International Conference on Software Engineering*, 2005. 31

[62] J. Kephart and S. White. A Research Agenda for Business-driven Information Technology. In *HotAC I: Hot Topics in Autonomic Computing*, 2005. 32, 33

[63] D. E. Knuth. *Art of Computer Programming, Volume 1: Fundamental Algorithms*. Addison-Wesley Professional, November 1969. 80, 86

[64] S. Krishnan, P. Wagstrom, and G. von Laszewski. GSFL: A Workflow Framework for Grid Services, 2002. http://www-unix.mcs.anl.gov/ laszewsk/bib/papers/vonLaszewski-gsfl-a.pdf. 5, 8

[65] K. Lee, R. Sakellariou, N. Paton, and A. Fernandes. Workflow Adaptation as an Autonomic Computing Problem. In *WORKS '07: Proceedings of the 2nd Workshop on Workflows in Support of Large-scale Science*, 2007. 33

[66] C. Lekkerkerker and J. Boland. Representation of a Finite Graph by a Set of Intervals on the Real Line. *Fundamenta Mathematicae*, 51:45–64, 1962. 88

[67] C. Letondal. A Web Interface Generator for Molecular Biology Programs in Unix. *Bioinformatics*, 17(1):73–82, 2001. 13

[68] F. Leymann. Web Services: Distributed Applications without Limits. In *BPM '03: Proceedings of the International Conference on Business Process Management*, 2003. 31

[69] F. Leymann, D. Roller, and M.-T. Schmidt. Web Services and Business Process Management. *IBM Systems Journal*, 41(2):198–211, 2002. 5, 31

[70] D. Liu and M. Franklin. GridDB: A Data-Centric Overlay for Scientific Grids. In *VLDB '04: Proceedings of the 30st International Conference on Very Large Data Bases*, 2004. 80, 82, 111

[71] G. P. Liu and S. Daley. Optimal-tuning PID Control for Industrial Systems. *Control Engineering Practice*, 9(11):1185–1194, November 2001. 67

[72] S. J. Ludtke, P. R. Baldwin, and W. Chiu. EMAN: Semiautomated Software for High-Resolution Single-Particle Reconstructions. *Journal of Structural Biology*, 128(1):82–97, December 1999. 83, 102

Bibliography

[73] T. Maguire and D. Snelling. Web Services Service Group 1.2, June 2004. http://docs.oasis-open.org/wsrf/wsrf-ws-service-group-1.2-spec-pr-01.pdf. 9

[74] K. M. McCann, M. Yarrow, A. DeVivo, and P. Mehrotra. ScyFlow: An Environment for the Visual Specification and Execution of Scientific Workflows. In *GGF10: Proceedings of GGF10 Workflow in Grid Systems*, Berlin, Germany, 2004. 8

[75] R. McClatchey, J.-M. L. Goff, N. Baker, W. Harris, and Z. Kovacs. *A Distributed Workflow and Product Data Management Application for the Construction of Large Scale Scientific Apparatus*. NATO ASI Series. Springer, 1997. 31

[76] R. M. McConnell and J. P. Spinrad. Modular Decomposition and Transitive Orientation. *Discrete Mathematics*, 201(1-3):189–241, 1999. 88

[77] J. Meidanis, G. Vossen, and M. Weske. Using Workflow Management in DNA Sequencing. In *CoopIS '96: Proceedings of the 1st International Conference on Cooperative Information Systems*, June 1996. 31

[78] D. A. Menascé and M. N. Bennani. On the Use of Performance Models to Design Self-Managing Computer Systems. In *CMG '03: Proceedings of Computer Measurement Group Conference*, 2003. 33

[79] S. Miles, E. Deelman, P. Groth, K. Vahi, G. Mehta, and L. Moreau. Connecting Scientific Data to Scientific Experiments with Provenance. In *e-Science '07: Proceedings of the third IEEE International Conference on e-Science and Grid Computing*, 2007. 82, 107

[80] S. Miles, P. Groth, M. Branco, and L. Moreau. The Requirements of Using Provenance in e-Science Experiments. *Journal of Grid Computing*, 5:1–25, 2005. 80

[81] G.-J. Na and S.-W. Lee. A Relational Nested Interval Encoding Scheme for XML Storage and Retrieval. In *Information Retrieval Technology* Springer Berlin / Heidelberg, 2005. 86, 111

[82] A. I. Nesvizhskii and R. Aebersold. Interpretation of Shotgun Proteomic Data: The Protein Inference Problem. *Molecular Cell Proteomics*, 4(10):1419–1440, 2005. 105

[83] P. Nibblet and S. Graham. Events and Service-oriented Architecture: The OASIS Web Services Notification Specifications. *IBM Systems Journal: Service-Oriented Architecture*, 44(4):869–886, 2005. 5

[84] J. Norris, K. Coleman, A. Fox, and G. Candea. OnCall: Defeating Spikes with a Free-Market Application Cluster. In *ICAC'04: Proceedings of the 2nd International Conference on Autonomic Computing*, 2004. 31

[85] P. Obreiter and G. Graef. Towards scalability in tuple spaces. In *SAC '02: Proceedings of the 17th ACM Symposium on Applied Computing*, 2002. 37

[86] T. Oinn, M. Greenwood, M. Addis, M. N. Alpdemir, J. Ferris, K. Glover, C. Goble, A. Goderis, D. Hull, D. Marvin, P. Li, P. Lord, M. R. Pocock, M. Senger, R. Stevens, A. Wipat, and C. Wroe. Taverna: Lessons in Creating a Workflow Environment for the Life Sciences. *Concurrency and Computation: Practice & Experience*, 18(10):1067–1100, 2006. 80

[87] J. Parekh, G. Kaiser, P. Gross, and G. Valetto. Retrofitting Autonomic Capabilities onto Legacy Systems. *Cluster Computing*, 9(2):141–159, 2006. 31

[88] C. Pautasso. JOpera: Process Support for more than Web services. http://www.jopera.org. 15, 31, 80

[89] C. Pautasso and G. Alonso. From Web Service Composition to Megaprogramming. In *TES-04: Proceedings of the 5th VLDB Workshop on Technologies for E-Services*, 2004. 35

[90] C. Pautasso and G. Alonso. The JOpera Visual Composition Language. *Journal of Visual Languages and Computing*, 16(1–2):119–152, 2004. 8, 15

[91] C. Pautasso and G. Alonso. JOpera: a Toolkit for Efficient Visual Composition of Web Services. *International Journal of Electronic Commerce*, 9(2):104–141, 2004/2005. 33, 37

[92] C. Pautasso and G. Alonso. Flexible Binding for Reusable Composition of Web Services. In *SC '05: Proceedings of the 4th Workshop on Software Composition*, 2005. 5

[93] C. Pautasso, T. Heinis, and G. Alonso. Autonomic Execution of Web Service Compositions. In *ICWS '05: Proceedings of the 3rd IEEE International Conference on Web Services*, 2005. 2, 6, 31

[94] D. N. Perkins, D. J. C. Pappin, D. M. Creasy, and J. S. Cottrell. Probability Based Protein Identification By Searching Sequence Databases Using Mass Spectrometry Data. *Electrophoresis*, 20(18):3551–3567, 1999. 105

[95] A. Pnueli, A. Lempel, and S. Even. Transitive Orientation of Graphs and Identification of Permutation Graphs. *Canadian Journal of Mathematics*, 23:160–175, 1971. 88, 92, 116

[96] R. Rifaieh, R. Unwin, J. Carver, and M. A. Miller. SWAMI: Integrating Biological Databases and Analysis Tools Within User Friendly Environment. In *Data Integration in the Life Sciences*, volume 4544 of *Lecture Notes in Computer Science*. Springer, 2007. 83

[97] S. Sanjeepan, A. Matsunaga, L. Zhu, H. Lam, and J. A. B. Fortes. A Service-Oriented, Scalable Approach to Grid-Enabling of Legacy Scientific Applications. In *ICWS '05: Proceedings of the International Conference on Web Services*, 2005. 7

Bibliography

[98] A. Schmidt, T. Sindt, M. Tepegoez, and G. Joeris. FlowTEC - An Information System Supporting Virtual Enterprises. In *CME'99: Proceedings of the 2nd International Conference on Concurrent Multidisciplinary Engineering*, 1999. 31

[99] K. Seymour, A. YarKhan, S. Agrawal, and J. Dongarra. NetSolve: Grid Enabling Scientific Computing Environments. In *Grid Computing and New Frontiers of High Performance Processing*. 2005. 83

[100] M. Shaw. Self-Healing: Softening Precision to Avoid Brittleness. In *WOSS '02: Proceedings of the 1st Workshop on Self-Healing Systems*, 2002. 41

[101] B. A. Shirazi, A. R. Hurson, and K. M. Kavi, editors. *Scheduling and Load Balancing in Parallel and Distributed Systems*. IEEE Computer Society Press, 1995. 33

[102] Y. L. Simmhan, B. Plale, and D. Gannon. A Survey of Data Provenance in e-Science. *SIGMOD Record*, 34(3):31–36, 2005. 80

[103] Y. L. Simmhan, B. Plale, and D. Gannon. A Framework for Collecting Provenance in Data-Centric Scientific Workflows. In *ICWS '06: Proceedings of the IEEE International Conference on Web Services*, 2006. 82, 107

[104] S. W. Sorde, S. K. Aggarwal, J. Song, M. Koh, and S. See. Modeling and Verifying Non-DAG Workflows for Computational Grids. *IEEE Congress on Services*. 83, 102

[105] F. Stefan. 3-Interval Irreducible Partially Ordered Sets. *Order*, 11(12):97–125, 1994. 88

[106] E. Stolte and G. Alonso. Efficient Exploration of Large Scientific Databases. In *VLDB '02: Proceedings of the 28th International Conference on Very Large Data Bases*, 2002. 80

[107] E. Stolte, C. von Praun, G. Alonso, and T. Gross. Scientific Data Repositories - Designing for a Moving Target. In *SIGMOD '03: Proceedings of the 28th ACM SIGMOD International Conference on Management of Data*, 2003. 80

[108] I. Taylor, M. Shields, I. Wang, and A. Harrison. The Triana Workflow Environment: Architecture and Applications. In *Workflows for e-Science*. Springer, 2007. 80

[109] I. Taylor, M. Shields, I. Wang, and O. Rana. Triana Applications within Grid Computing and Peer to Peer Environments. *Journal of Grid Computing*, 1(2):199–217, 2003. 8

[110] M. Tedder, D. Corneil, M. Habib, and C. Paul. Simpler Linear-Time Modular Decomposition Via Recursive Factorizing Permutations. *Automata, Languages and Programming*, 2008. 116

Bibliography

[111] S. Trissl and U. Leser. Fast and Practical Indexing and Querying of Very Large Graphs. In *SIGMOD '07: Proceedings of the 32nd ACM SIGMOD International Conference on Management of Data*, 2007. 81, 114

[112] V. Tropashko. Nested Intervals Tree Encoding in SQL. *SIGMOD Record*, 34(2):47–52, 2005. 86, 111

[113] W. T. Trotter and J. I. Moore. Characterization Problems for Graphs, Partially Ordered Sets, Lattices and Families of Sets. *Discrete Mathematics*, 16:361–381, 1976. 88

[114] J. R. Ullmann. An Algorithm for Subgraph Isomorphism. *Journal of the ACM*, 23(1):31–42, 1976. 89

[115] W. Vambenepe. Web Services Base Topics 1.2, June 2004. http://docs.oasis-open.org/wsn/2004/06/wsn-WS-Topics-1.2-draft-01.pdf. 9

[116] W. M. P. van der Aalst. Process-oriented Architectures for Electronic Commerce and Interorganizational Workflow. *Information Systems*, 24(8):639–671, December 1999. 31

[117] W. M. P. van der Aalst, A. H. M. ter Hofstede, B. Kiepuszewski, and A. P. Barros. Workflow Patterns. *Distributed and Parallel Databases*, 14(3):5–51, July 2003. 93

[118] H. Veregin and D. Lanter. Data Quality Enhancement Techniques in Layer-Based Geographic Information Systems. *Computers, Environment and Urban Systems*, 19:23–36(14), 1995. 80

[119] G. von Laszewski. Java CoG Kit Workflow Concepts for Scientific Experiments, 2005. http://www-unix.mcs.anl.gov/ laszewsk/papers/vonLaszewski-workflow-taylor-anl.pdf. 8

[120] H. Wang, H. He2, J. Yang, P. S. Yu, and J. X. Yu. Dual Labeling: Answering Graph Reachability Queries in Constant Time. In *ICDE '06: Proceedings of the 22nd International Conference on Data Engineering*, 2006. 81, 113

[121] G. Weikum, A. Moenkeberg, C. Hasse, and P. Zabback. Self-tuning Database Technology and Information Services: from Wishful Thinking to Viable Engineering. In *VLDB '02: Proceedings of the 8th International Conference on Very Large Data Bases*, 2002. 33

[122] E. Wolk. A Note on the Comparability Graph of a Tree. *Proceedings of the American Mathematical Society*, 16(1):17–20, February 1965. 88

[123] M. Yannakakis. The Complexity of the Partial Order Dimension Problem. *SIAM Journal on Algebraic and Discrete Methods*, 3(3):351–358, 1982. 88

Bibliography

[124] J. R. Yates, J. K. Eng, A. L. McCormack, and D. Schieltz. Method to Correlate Tandem Mass Spectra of Modified Peptides to Amino Acid Sequences in the Protein Database. *Analytical Chemistry*, 67(8):1426–1436, 1995. 105

[125] J. Yu and R. Buyya. A Novel Architecture for Realizing Grid Workflow using Tuple Spaces. In *Grid 2004: Proceedings of the 5th International Workshop on Grid Computing*, 2004. 8

[126] L.-J. Zhang and M. Jeckle. The Next Big Thing: Web services Collaboration. In *ICWS-Europe 2003: Proceedings of the International Conference on Web Services*, 2003. 31

[127] J. Ziegler and N. Nichols. Optimum Settings for Automatic Controllers. *ASME Transactions*, 64:759–768, November 1942. 66

yes
I want morebooks!

Buy your books fast and straightforward online - at one of the world's fastest growing online book stores! Environmentally sound due to Print-on-Demand technologies.

Buy your books online at
www.get-morebooks.com

Kaufen Sie Ihre Bücher schnell und unkompliziert online – auf einer der am schnellsten wachsenden Buchhandelsplattformen weltweit!
Dank Print-On-Demand umwelt- und ressourcenschonend produziert.

Bücher schneller online kaufen
www.morebooks.de

OmniScriptum Marketing DEU GmbH
Heinrich-Böcking-Str. 6-8
D - 66121 Saarbrücken
Telefax: +49 681 93 81 567-9

info@omniscriptum.com
www.omniscriptum.com

Printed by Books on Demand GmbH, Norderstedt / Germany